Melville: The Ironic Diagram

Melville:
The Ironic Diagram

JOHN SEELYE

NORTHWESTERN UNIVERSITY PRESS

EVANSTON

1970

John Seelye is Associate Professor of English
at the University
of Connecticut.

"If circumstances lead me, I will find
Where truth is hid, though it were hid indeed
Within the center."

Hamlet

Contents

Note on Texts

Until the projected Northwestern-Newberry Edition of Melville's writings is completed, the textual situation will remain chaotic, as the following list of citations indicates. In each instance I have cited the text which usage and experience have dictated is the most reliable. The great exception to this are the volumes in the Constable Edition, which are notoriously unreliable, but nonetheless "standard."

References to *Typee: A Peep at Polynesian Life* are to the Northwestern-Newberry Edition, vol. 1 of *The Writings of Herman Melville,* ed. Harrison Hayford, Hershel Parker, and G. Thomas Tanselle, with a Historical Note by Leon Howard, Northwestern University Press and The Newberry Library (Evanston and Chicago, 1968).

References to *Omoo: A Narrative of Adventures in the South Seas* are to the Northwestern-Newberry Edition, vol. 2 of *The Writings of Herman Melville,* ed. Harrison Hayford, Hershel Parker, and G. Thomas Tanselle, with a Historical Note by Gordon Roper, Northwestern University Press and The Newberry Library (Evanston and Chicago, 1968).

References to *Mardi* are to the Northwestern-Newberry Edition, Vol. 3 of *The Writings of Herman Melville,* ed. Harrison Hayford, Hershel Parker, and G. Thomas Tanselle, with a Historical Note by Elizabeth S. Foster, Northwestern University Press and The Newberry Library (Evanston and Chicago, 1969).

References to *Redburn: His First Voyage* are to the Northwestern-Newberry Edition, vol. 4 of *The Writings of Herman Melville,* ed. Harrison Hayford, Hershel Parker, and G. Thomas Tanselle, with a Historical Note by Hershel Parker, Northwestern University Press and The Newberry Library (Evanston and Chicago, 1969).

References to *White-Jacket* are to the Northwestern-Newberry Edition, Vol. 5 of *The Writings of Herman Melville,* ed. Harrison Hayford, Hershel Parker, and G. Thomas Tanselle, with a Historical Note by Willard Thorpe, Northwestern University Press and The Newberry Library (Evanston and Chicago, 1969).

References to *Moby-Dick: or, The Whale,* are to the Hendricks House Edition, ed. Luther S. Mansfield and Howard P. Vincent (New York, 1952); as are references to *Pierre: or, The Ambiguities,* ed. Henry A. Murray (New York, 1949, 1957); *The Confidence-Man: His Masquerade,* ed. Elizabeth S. Foster (New York, 1954); *Collected Poems,* ed. Howard P. Vincent (Chicago, 1947); and *Clarel: A Poem and Pilgrimage in the Holy Land,* ed. Walter E. Bezanson (New York, 1960).

References to *Billy Budd* are to *Billy Budd, Sailor (An Inside Narrative),* ed. Harrison Hayford and Merton M. Sealts, Jr. (Chicago, 1962). References to the short stories and sketches are to *Selected Writings of Herman Melville* (New York, 1952). References to the *Battle-Pieces and Aspects of the War* are to *The Battle-Pieces of Herman Melville,* ed. Hennig Cohen (New York, 1963). References to "Fragments from a Writing Desk, No. 2," are to "Appendix B" of William H. Gilman's *Melville's Early Life and Redburn* (New

York, 1951). References to "Daniel Orme" are to "Appendix I" of *Melville's Billy Budd,* ed. F. Barron Freeman (Cambridge, Mass., 1948).

Other works that are cited are: *The Letters of Herman Melville,* ed. Merrell R. Davis and William H. Gilman (New Haven, 1960); Jay Leyda, *The Melville Log: A Documentary Life of Herman Melville, 1819–1891* (New York, 1951); *Herman Melville: Representative Selections,* ed. Willard Thorp (New York, 1938); and *Journal of a Visit to London and the Continent,* ed. Eleanor Melville Metcalf (Cambridge, Mass., 1948).

All other references are to the "Standard Edition" of *The Works of Herman Melville,* ed. Raymond M. Weaver (London, 1922–24; reissued in facsimile, New York, 1963), the aforementioned "Constable Edition."

To keep the apparatus to a minimum, I have not included page references to the short stories and poems, since these citations are relatively easy to locate.

Bibliographical Note

Rather than clutter what follows with an apparatus of footnotes, I should like here to list the critical and scholarly works on Herman Melville and the general topic of irony which I have consulted during the ten years involved in the completion of this study.

The discussion of Melville's romantic irony, in Chapter I, "The Ironic Diagram," is based primarily on Augustus William Schlegel, *A Course of Lectures on Dramatic Art and Literature,* trans. John Black (Philadelphia, 1833); and Samuel Taylor Coleridge, *The Complete Works of Samuel Taylor Coleridge,* ed. W. G. T. Shedd (New York, 1854), vol. 4, *Notes and Lectures upon Shakespeare,* ed. Mrs. H. N. Coleridge. These translations and texts have been chosen because of their availability to Melville. I have also found valuable explications and definitions of romantic irony in Irving Babbitt's chapter, "Romantic Irony," in *Rousseau and Romanticism* (New York: Meridian Books, 1955); in Alfred E. Lussky's *Tieck's Romantic Irony: With Special Emphasis Upon the Influence of Cervantes, Sterne, and Goethe* (Chapel Hill, N.C., 1932); and in René Wellek's chapters, "Friedrich Schlegel," and "August Wilhelm Schlegel," in *A History of Modern Criticism: 1750–1950* (New Haven, 1955), vol. 2, *The Romantic Age.*

Further significant references to Melville's use of irony may be found in Charles Feidelson, Jr., *Symbolism and American Literature* (Chicago, 1953); Northrop Frye, *Anatomy of Criticism* (Princeton, 1957); and Edwin Honig, *Dark Conceit: The Making of Allegory* (Cambridge, Mass., 1960).

Works of criticism which have treated various aspects of Melville's use of irony are Richard Harter Fogle, *Melville's Shorter Tales* (Norman, Okla., 1960); Edward H. Rosenberry, *Melville and the Comic Spirit* (Cambridge, Mass., 1955); and Lawrance Thompson, *Melville's Quarrel With God* (Princeton, 1952), a work to which I owe much and with which I differ considerably. I should like particularly to call attention to Thompson's running discussion of Melville and Carlyle in his footnotes, an important assist to an understanding of Melville's romantic irony.

Discussions relevant to individual works may be found in Merrell Davis, *Melville's Mardi: A Chartless Voyage* (New Haven, 1952); Elizabeth Foster, Introduction to *The Confidence-Man* (New York, 1954); and Jay Leyda, Introduction to *The Complete Stories of Herman Melville* (New York, 1949).

No study of Melville's structures can escape confrontation with his use of the quest pattern. The two works to which I am particularly indebted, and which best serve to define my own position, are Merlin Bowen, *The Long Encounter: Self and Experience in the Writings of Herman Melville* (Chicago, 1960); and Milton R. Stern, *The Fine Hammered Steel of Herman Melville* (Urbana, Ill., 1957).

As this study was entering its final stage of revision, there appeared Paul Brodtkorb, Jr.'s *Ishmael's White World: A Phenomenological Study of Moby-Dick* (New Haven, 1965), a book which, though approaching *Moby-Dick* from a different direction, verified much that I have to say about that novel. Though not indebted to Mr. Brodtkorb, I am certainly grateful to him.

It remains to be said that Chapter I, "The Ironic Diagram," is a revised version of an essay by the same title which appeared in *The Recognition of Herman Melville*, ed. Hershel Parker (Ann Arbor, 1967), pp. 347–64, and that portions of Chapter V appeared in different form as "The Golden Navel: The Cabalism of Ahab's Doubloon," *Nineteenth-Century Fiction*, XIV (1960), 350–55.

Chapter One

The Ironic Diagram

The decline of Melville's reputation during his lifetime was assisted by the equivocalness of style and structure found in his most ambitious works. In *Mardi*, *Moby-Dick*, *Pierre*, and *The Confidence-Man*, Melville seems to be speaking from a cloud of self-conscious obfuscation, which, along with the implications of meaning detected behind that cloud, alienated him from the readers of his own day. As tastes changed, as ambiguity became accepted, even prized as a means of artistic expression, Melville's reputation improved, first through rediscovery of *Moby-Dick*, then because of reappraisal of *Pierre*, and in the last decade with realization of the importance of *The Confidence-Man*, the most obscure and difficult of the novels published during his lifetime. By now, a generation of critics has attempted to discern patterns of consistency in Melville's works, has tried to show that the many indirections meet at a common point. Yet, perhaps because each attempt has been predicably shaped by the personality or politics of the individual "reader," the cloud remains essentially undispelled—though undoubtedly made more colorful by the subjective images projected upon it. Like the whale who bears the name, *Moby-Dick* remains a mystery, an oracle without a sybil.

Perhaps this is as it should be. There may be *no* solution to the mystery, for Melville's ambiguity may be the result of the restless search for a "definite belief" which Hawthorne attributed to him. The only way to be sure is to solve the enigma of Melville himself, a man who, even in his letters and journals, is a Proteus of psychological and philosophical changes. To derive consistency from his letters, as from his novels and poems, is to impose it upon them. Which returns us again to the possibility that Melville could not or would not make up his mind, that he was impelled by his uncertainties to create forms which would encompass them.

The direction of his reading during the formative years between *Typee* and *Moby-Dick* reinforces this possibility. Lucian, Rabelais, Montaigne, Burton, and Bayle provided Melville with a library of Pyrrhonic writings, and the mingling of Byronic and Carlylean elements in *Moby-Dick* suggests as well a sympathy with the forms and attitudes of romantic irony, with its emphasis on doubt and disarray. The influence of romantic irony is also found in Melville's reading of Shakespeare, an interpretation derived from Coleridge and the brothers Schlegel. For those romantic critics, Shakespeare was a puzzlemaker, a magician of many faces and voices who fashioned mysteries, each partaking of the godlike inclusiveness of the author's self, but none revealing his true identity, the convictions of his "inkept" soul.

Much of what Melville had to say about the artistic process is abstracted from Coleridge and Schlegel—from his famous statement to Hawthorne about the "inmost leaf of the bulb" (*L*, p. 130) to the thought, voiced in *Pierre*, that "most grand productions of the best human intellects ever are built round a circle, as atolls . . . digestively including the whole range of all that can be known or dreamed" (p. 333). Melville shared with the romantic critics the conviction that a work of art should be all-inclusive, like "Lombardo's 'Koztanza'" (in *Mardi*), a unity of totality, an organic composite given order by the artist's "crowned and sceptered instinct" (*M*, p. 597). Form, for Melville, was the meeting and mating of "unlike things," the "contraries," the opposed "extremes" of universal creation (*RS*, pp. 365, 427). Like the romantics' Shakespeare, Melville championed paradox and mystery and sought out forms which would accommodate "universality of thought."

Take the problem of double consciousness in *Moby-Dick*, where two "voices" demand our attention: the heroic God-hatred of Ahab and Ishmael's companionable skepticism. The two attitudes meet on the common ground that there is a "wisdom that is woe," but whereas Ahab has carried his woe to an extreme, has hardened his heart against man, beast, and God, Ishmael realizes that there is also "a woe that is madness" and warns the reader against staring too long into the hell-fire of deepest doubt: "Give not thyself up, then, to fire, lest it invert thee, deaden thee" (p. 422). Both voices are invested with a weight of subjectiveness—the one through soliloquy, the other through a first-person address to the reader—and both have had their advocates among critics who have imposed an absolute interpretation on Melville's ambiguities.

Writing to Hawthorne, Melville championed the man "who declares himself a sovereign nature (in himself) amid the powers of heaven, hell, and earth. He may perish; but so long as he exists he insists upon treating with all Powers upon an equal basis. If any of those other Powers choose to withhold certain secrets, let them; that does not impair my sovereignty in myself; that does not make me tributary" (L, pp. 124–25). This was written in 1851, and it is apparent that the Faustian "he" (Hawthorne) and "me" (Melville) reflect the "he-and-I" of Ahab, whose sovereign self dominates Melville's greatest book. But in another letter to Hawthorne, Melville noted that "what plays the mischief with the truth is that all men will insist upon the universal application of a temporary feeling or opinion" (L, p. 131). Though he was talking about transcendental benevolence, Melville could as well have been describing his inverted Emersonian hero, that universal applicator, Captain Ahab. Ishmael, on the other hand, tempers his doubts and his delight with a saving skepticism.

Both Ahab and Ishmael are spokesmen for a troubled consciousness. Melville created in Ahab a Byronic figure to express his

profound pessimism about the goodness of divine purpose. In
Ishmael, he created a more complex vehicle, a voice which varies
from a sage appreciation of Solomon to a smug recommendation
of home and heart as man's best felicity. Melville could not be
completely an Ahab, nor could he subscribe to the excesses of
Ishmael's kind regard for the sunnier aspects of life, but both
voices serve as instruments to express his wanderings between
those antipodes of light and shadow. Like Coleridge's Don Quixote and Sancho Panza, they need each other. Separate but
inseparable, they are the creations of an artist who regarded his art
as a system of tensions produced by diagrammatic contrasts, a
symposium of opposed viewpoints.

Another aspect of Melville's craft derived from romantic attitudes toward Shakespeare is its stylistic indirection. With Coleridge, Melville felt that it was "through the mouths of the dark
characters of Hamlet, Timon, Lear, and Iago" that Shakespeare
"craftily says, or sometimes insinuates the things which we feel to
be so terrifically true, that it were all but madness for any good
man, in his own proper character, to utter, or even hint of them."
It is this "infinite obscure" that Melville most prized in Shakespeare, the "mystical blackness" which he also admired in Hawthorne, lurking behind the obscuring "Indian-summer sunlight"
on the near side of his soul. For Melville, Shakespeare and
Hawthorne were "masters of the great Art of Telling the Truth,—
even though it be covertly and by snatches" (RS: pp. 333–34).

Thus Ahab, like Lear, speaks the "sane madness of vital truth,"
while Ishmael's frequent expressions of sunny views often ring
false. Like Stubb, Ishmael is "one of those odd sort of humorists,
whose jollity is sometimes . . . curiously ambiguous" (MD, p.
217). Ahab's madness is a protective screen shielding Melville's
periodic bouts of oracular pessimism, while Ishmael's hyena laugh
is aimed, as one of Melville's contemporaries observed with distaste, at "the most sacred associations of life" (Log, I, 437). Ahab's
attention is centered on one obsessive goal, but Ishmael is ran-
domly discursive, concealing his skepticism by a flow of com-

panionable chatter. Through Ahab's "madness" and Ishmael's sly hints and nudges, Melville hoped to "insinuate" his "blackness . . . to those who may best understand it, and account for it; it is not obtruded upon every one alike" (RS, p. 335), a darkness not only of blasphemy but of doubt.

For a combination of contraries and contrariness suggests both isolation and uncertainty. There is no absolute center of value in Melville's work to which one may refer, no moral standpoint against which to measure the declarations of his characters. Where contrasting characterization in Shakespeare's plays suggests an affirmative balance, in Melville it is often paradoxical, mutually destructive. His use of stylistic indirection, shaped by diagrammatic confrontation, is similarly useless as a guide to intention. The same may be said of Melville's adaptation of the quest structure, the complex heritage of Spenser, Cervantes, Bunyan, Rabelais, Byron, and Shelley.

The diagrammatic opposition of character and opinion which Melville derived from the romantics' Shakespeare is relativistic in implication, all parts mutually contradicting one another. But the quest has absolute implications. It is, after all, a journey after or into *something*, even if that something turns out to be nothing after all. For Spenser, the veil of appearances conceals an absolute, Platonic reality; for Bunyan, it clouds the true road to heaven. For the romantics, on the other hand, reality is a mist concealing an absolute void: *Childe Harold* and *Alastor* provide a heritage of futility. What all quests have in common, however, is the forward thrust of inquiry, the dynamic assertion of self in a progressive line of exploration. In Spenser and Bunyan, this assertion results in wisdom and salvation. In the romantics, it results in annihilation, a Faustian finale. The romantic quester is ultimately mistaken in his search for an absolute, but the tragic heroism of his task is seldom questioned.

In adapting the linear implications of the quest to his purpose, Melville borrowed elements from all his predecessors: the imagery of Spenser, the allegory of Spenser and Bunyan, the satiric voyage of Rabelais, and the heroic, despairing questers of Byron and Shelley. But as Shakespeare dominated the influence of Montaigne, Burton, and Sir Thomas Browne, so Cervantes seems to have been the primary source of Melville's quest structures. Once again, Coleridge was the medium of transference, for Melville's Quixote, "that sagest sage that ever lived," is a mixture of heroism and folly, his quest nonetheless admirable for its ultimate futility. Captain Ahab, with his gaunt figure and his lance, is cast in Quixote's mold more than in Perseus', his mad idealism countered by Ishmael's Sancho Panza-like skepticism. Like the romantics' Quixote, Ahab is part parody, part tragic hero, a noble fool in pursuit of his own mad image, a madness that may contain the saneness of truth.

II

The structure of *Moby-Dick* may be seen as a diagrammatic opposition of forces, expressive of Melville's own conflict of belief. Thus Ahab's quest, his onrush towards the Whale, provides a kinetic, linear element—the "story." Counterpoised against this movement are the static, discursive cetology chapters, essays in skepticism given unity by Ishmael's insistence on the relativity of perception. Similar in function are the contrasting "ideas" about the Whale expressed by the chief members of the crew, a symposium of opinions supplemented by other ships which the *Pequod* encounters. Structural counterpoise in turn gives impulse to style, for Ahab speaks the rhetorical bombast of melodrama, while Ishmael prefers satire's sly mockery.

These patterns of static and kinetic elements may be figured as a line and circle. The line is associated with Ahab's kinesis, the circle with the various "rounds" of opinion, summed up by the relativistic roundness of the world itself, which turns the line of inquiry into a circle. Circular also is Ishmael's return trip of wisdom, as opposed to Ahab's voyage out of exploration, a roundness which corresponds to the world-wholeness of matched contraries and which gives the traveler a sage appreciation of relative values. There are times when Melville hints that the circle may be a Shakespearean *discordia concors,* a binding together of the disparate elements of the world in a harmonious whole that seems to contradict the straightforward, single-purposed intention of the quester. But there is found in these configurations, always, an image or allusion which calls the apparent harmony into question, which breaks the circle momentarily.

A good example is the episode in *Moby-Dick* in which Ishmael's boat glides through a circle of gallied whales into the calm of the inner circle, where "the storms in the roaring glens between the outermost whales were heard but not felt. . . . Yes, we were now in that enchanted calm which they say lurks at the heart of every commotion" (*MD*, pp. 384–85). Gazing down through the transparent waters within the circle, Ishmael sees a vision of motherhood and love protected from the stormy violence beyond the barrier: "Though surrounded by circle upon circle of consternations and affrights, did these inscrutable creatures at the centre freely and fearlessly indulge in all peaceful concernments; yea, serenely revelled in dalliance and delight" (p. 387).

This mystic circle of inner quietude bordered by strife seems to approximate the "All" that was Nature for the transcendentalists, a supernal peace which has its counterpart in the soul of man: "Amid the tornadoed Atlantic of my being, do I myself still for ever centrally disport in mute calm; and while ponderous planets of unwaning woe revolve round me, deep down and deep inland there I still bathe me in eternal mildness of joy." But Melville told Hawthorne that there was "an immense deal of flummery" in the "*all* feeling" (*L*, p. 131), and the harmony of the whale circle is broken when a lone animal, maimed (like Ahab) and in agony, dashes "among the revolving circles" and brings the "entire host of whales . . . tumbling upon their inner centre." Flux, not stasis, is the true condition of Nature, and doubts, similarly, invade the serenity of the deepest soul. However peaceful may be the inner garden of contentment, no man may abide there forever.

This process of endless qualification is intrinsic to the planetary arrangement of forces in Melville's diagram. In *Moby-Dick,* the emphasis is on the outer circle, the sphere of hatred, storms, affrights. Perhaps to counter what he may have felt was the obstinate optimism of his contemporaries, Melville used light chiefly to emphasize the blackness of darkness. Bobbing to the surface at the end of the catastrophe, Ishmael undergoes a resurrection which qualifies in turn the destruction of Ahab and his ship, but he is saved by clinging to a universal symbol of death, and he rises in the midst of a swirling vortex of annihilation. The spreading ring of foam that marks the grave of the *Pequod* is a circle of emptiness, the equivalent of Moby Dick's massive blankness. Both are the expressions of mystery, which becomes Mystery as the bulk of the Whale resolves into a spreading circle of nothingness.

"Perhaps, after all," Melville wrote to Hawthorne (and the qualifying "perhaps" has much meaning), "there is *no* secret," no ultimate key to the mystery of existence: "We incline to think that the Problem of the Universe is like the Freemason's mighty secret, so terrible to all children. It turns out, at last, to consist in a triangle, a mallet, and an apron,—nothing more!" (*L,* p. 125). The world may be a void, masked by appearances, but—and it is here that Melville's will to believe somehow keeps him from complete nihilism and ends *Moby-Dick* with an Epilogue of resurrection—we must acknowledge our own existence. "It is this *Being* of the matter," he declared to Hawthorne, "there lies the knot with which we choke ourselves. As soon as you say Me, a God, a Nature, so soon you jump off from your stool and hang from the beam." If a Gordian knot much like this puts an end to Ahab's mad quest, which is an ultimate extension of Emersonian self-reliance, it is Ishmael's ability to confront such a knot with an ironic equanimity which brings *him* through without harm. An equilibrist, Ishmael makes it across safely, dancing along the rope which strangles Captain Ahab.

If Melville's questers are persistent in their settings-forth, that persistence is quixotic, for all are ultimately baffled by the confusing contradictoriness of a world which has "no secret," no absolute basis. Empathizing with his outward-moving heroes, yet aware of their essential fallibility, Melville uses them to explore the shifting, relativistic territory of Truth, a journey which necessarily spirals down into the maelstrom of ultimate mystery. "For things visible are but conceits of the eye: things imaginative, conceits of the fancy. If duped by one, we are equally duped by the other." To the "old interrogatory . . . what is truth?" there is no answer not in the question (M, p. 284). But the urgent necessity of that question and the possibility of that answer dictate the dimensions of Melville's ironic diagram, the Euclidian expression of truth towards which his art is aimed.

Melville's work, after *Moby-Dick*, has been seen as stages of increasing bitterness, culminating in the emphasis on despair and death in *Clarel*. In his last poems and *Billy Budd*, however, many readers have detected an atmosphere of hope, acceptance, or acquiescence. Certainly the disappearance of the heroic quester in Melville's last novels and short stories, along with his abandoning the romance for satire, is a sign of a sort, as is the increasing emphasis on natural images of flowering growth and resurrection in his final writings. And yet, considering the implications of even his most dynamic quests, there is not much difference between *Moby-Dick* and *The Confidence-Man*, *Pierre* and *Billy Budd*. Both *Moby-Dick* and *Clarel* end with an optimistic note, with a "swimmer rising from the deep," and in *Billy Budd* extremes of being are confronted by another equilibrist reader of Montaigne.

Most of Melville's structures involve a planetary balance of forces, in which the narrative thrust—the forward movement of a quest—is countered by a system of paradoxical contrasts. Epical counterpoise in *Moby-Dick*, satiric equipoise in *The Confidence-Man*, this symposiumlike arrangement of possibilities is consistently ironic, an ambiguous diagram found throughout Melville's writings. In *Moby-Dick*, the forward thrust of inquiry appears to dominate the structure, but proportionately it is only one part of the diagram; in *The Confidence-Man,* where the system of ironic contrasts lacks the epical dimension (and rhapsodic style) of Ahab's voyage out, the arrangement reaches a near standstill. Commencing with *Typee,* where Tommo's expectations are frustrated by the realities of native life, this diagram of ironic contrasts persists through the many changes of narrative form and style that mark the course of Melville's artistic development, ending with his last, uncompleted work, where the personality of Captain Vere is at once a tour de force of stylistic indirection and a psychomachia of diagrammatic conflict.

Truth, for Melville, is a question, not an answer, and by abandoning the answers imposed on existence by his questers, he only the more emphasized the final question. The emergence of Melville's final style, which is not the baroque rodomontade of *Moby-Dick* or the mannered irony of *The Confidence-Man* but is rather a hesitant, inquiring, parenthetical, and qualified syntax—a circling interrogation mark without a period, perfectly suits the revised proportions of his diagram. It suggests that if Melville had at last come to some terms with Mystery, he celebrated that final acquiescence by withdrawing behind mysteries of his own. The "inside narrative" has stories yet within, where the author remains concealed, perhaps undecided still, perhaps smiling—like Burton in his Oxford hermitage—at the heated urgency of those who would impose their own images on an eternal flux.

Chapter Two

Typee: The Quixotic Pattern

Melville's diagrammatic structure is evident in his earliest work—not only in *Typee,* but in a sketch written by him before setting out on the voyage that was to furnish the materials of his maritime romances. This "Fragment from a Writing Desk," the second of two pieces written in 1839, is a tale about a young man who is handed a love letter by a mysterious, cloaked figure whom he follows into a deep forest grove in search of the anonymous admirer. The messenger leads him to an Arabian-Gothic palace, which the youth enters with difficulty, to discover a voluptuous "Andalusian" princess awaiting him. At first enraptured by his discovery, he recoils in horror when he realizes that the beautiful girl is deaf and dumb, and the story ends on this note of ghastly disillusionment.

The oriental setting of the "Fragment," along with the luring cynosure and an enthusiastic plunge into erotic mystery, are devices basic to the romantic quest, as in Shelley's *Alastor.* Elements characteristic of Melville's later quests are also present here, moreover. Like Tommo, Taji, and Ishmael, the narrator sets out on his journey because of a psychological malaise (here, ennui), and the nature and fatal climax of his quest are suggested by a pattern of images and allusions, the materials with which Melville creates his ironic terrain. Promoting expectation, they also suggest ultimate futility and culminate in a sudden, painful conclusion.

A bored student, not a calm-beset or landlocked sailor, the narrator of the "Fragment" commences his quest by throwing aside his Greek lexicon and sallying forth "into the clear air of heaven." He soon encounters the mysterious messenger and is led through a pagan territory keyed by the dry contents of the lexicon. First there is a mysterious circle-in-a-grove, with a vaulted roof of leaves which seems "to have canopied the triumphal feasts of the sylvan god," a pagan allusion which has a counterpart in the paintings which decorate the chamber in which the student meets his maimed princess, "illustrative of the loves of Jupiter and Semele, Psyche before the tribunal of Venus, and a variety of other scenes." The princess herself is dressed in pink satin embroidered with "figures of Cupid in the act of drawing his bow," and she wears a bracelet of rubies, each representing an arrow-pierced heart. The allusions are overwhelmingly Ovidian, and the boredom of the student is replaced by a lover's ecstasy.

But the paintings on the wall refer to mortals who perished or almost perished because of their love for supernatural beings, and the room is furnished with large mirrors which multiply the furnishings, mirrors which also "deceived the eye by their reflections, and mocked the vision with long perspective," a suggestion of the illusory appearances which lure the student into assurance of bliss he is never to attain. Emphasizing artifice, the machinery of deception is Spenserian, adapted to the purposes of romantic disenchantment. The room is a Victorian version of Acrasia's bower, and the young student falls into the trap, to be stunned into truth by silence.

Silence, for Melville, is a thematic equivalent of his many circles, for like them it is a token of mystery which suggests the possibility of ultimate nothingness, the "trick" of the universe. "The last wisdom is dumb," declares Babbalanja, and at the Beginning there was an "Ineffable Silence, proceeding from its unimaginable remoteness" (M, pp. 620, 230). Silence attends

Pierre's departure from Saddle Meadows, it invests the snow-white bulk of Moby Dick with added awe, it is figured in the deaf mute whose advent commences *The Confidence-Man,* and it attends the execution of Billy Budd, whose fate is involved with a flaw of silence. Melville knew that silence was for the ancient Greeks "the vestibule to the higher mysteries," was aware of Carlyle's obsession with silence, and was deeply affected by its power himself, regarding it as "a strange thing," the correlative of emptiness and loneliness, containing the inexpressible implication of infinitude (*JVLC,* p. 48).

When Tommo at last discovers the hidden valley of the Typees, he is first dazzled by the whiteness of the thatched houses, then awestruck by the valley's "hushed repose," itself a counterpart to "the fearful silence" of the "unbroken solitude" at the island's interior (*T,* pp. 49, 44). Awesome also is the mysterious silence of the birds in the valley, whose "dumb beauty" always oppressed Tommo with "melancholy" (pp. 215–16), and his narrow escape from death at the hands of Mow-Mow is preceded by "profound silence" (p. 245). The implication of silence there is similar to what it is in the later novels, and though *Typee is without the symbolic complexity* of *Moby-Dick* or even *Mardi,* it is an elaboration in many ways on the materials of quest and consequent disillusionment found in the early "Fragment."

In place of the oriental trumpery found in the "Fragment" is the exotic background of the South Seas, and though Tommo is no student, he is a surprisingly cultured sailor. The nautical persona here established was to provide Melville with a narrative basis for a number of novels, but as the "Fragment" suggests, the fact of the sailor-author is almost incidental to the questing impulse that gives his narratives their characteristic form. *Typee,* like all the works to follow, is a variation on a pattern that was as familiar to Melville as his family Bible. To a consciousness weaned on Bunyan and Spenser, nourished on Byron and Shelley, and sated with Rabelais and Cervantes, the quest would be a mode of expression as natural as his mother tongue. The futility of the quest in the

"Fragment," as a quest less fatal than Taji's or Ahab's, suggests that, if Melville's maritime experience provided him with material for an American epic, it did little to shape the essential structure which that epic assumed.

II

Though *Typee* was presumably based on Melville's adventures on Nukuheva, the form is the romantic quest, with the familiar devices of an illusory basis, action inspired by boredom and a promise of paradise, a consequent penetration into a mystery, subsequent disillusionment, and an eventual retreat to the "real" world. If the "Fragment" mirrors *Alastor*, *Typee* takes its pattern from Scott's Waverley Novels. Ultimately inspired by Cervantes, this quixotic pattern is one of intellectual stripping and reeducation, of introducing a romance-fed youth into the realities of life as it is found. Romantic in atmosphere, it is anti-romance in purpose, with an ironic emphasis on countering dreams with hard fact.

Tommo is typically quixotic, a wandering Waverley who knows nothing about the South Seas except what he has heard and read, a guidebook and tall-tale miscellany of attractions and frights. Native girls are "houris" culled from the *Arabian Nights,* and the islands are generalized "groves," "blue waters," and "savage woodlands" (*T*, p. 5). But the islands of the South Seas turn out not to be the arcadia of low-lying country that he has imagined from his reading. He soon discovers them to be steep and mountainous, a wilderness of forests and towering cliffs. Furthermore, he finds little enough of paradise—at least on first encounter—for civilization has come to the South Seas, and the idealized natives of his dreams have been hopelessly corrupted by their contact with commerce. The pilot who guides the *Dolly* into the bay is a drunken English derelict, and the sailors' first sight of the islanders is a tangled confusion of merchant canoes vying with each other in an attempt to reach the American ship. A group of swimming native girls is first mistaken by Tommo for a school of fish, then, when he realizes his mistake, likened to mermaids. Clinging to the *Dolly,* "sparkling with savage vivacity, laughing gaily at one another, and chattering away with infinite glee," they seem the very type of primitive innocence, but once aboard the ship, the girls undergo a final metamorphosis. "Not the feeblest barrier was interposed between the unholy passions of the crew and their unlimited gratification" (pp. 14–15).

Undiscouraged by what he has witnessed, untutored by the demonstration of illusoriness, Tommo continues to be inspired by the accounts he has read of the islands. On the *Dolly,* all is known—life is sterile, routine, fixed. The island beyond the bay stands for all that is unknown, its emerald foliage mocking the flat green color with which the ship's bulwarks are painted. Although they reverse the imagery of the first chapter of *Moby-Dick,* the passages describing Tommo's discontent are motivated by the same idea. There, the inhabitants of the island city, Manhattan, yearn for the open sea; here, even the beams and planks of the ship seem to yearn for the shore. The whaler, in *Moby-Dick* a vessel of adventure, aimed for the voyage out, is here an ark of boredom, a contrast to the lure of the mysterious island beyond.

Tommo jumps ship with Toby, a daredevil youth ideally suited to an adventurous quest after a hidden valley and the first of several "companions" who appear in Melville's novels. An elaboration upon the "squire" figure in romances and the picaresque novel, like Queequeg he serves as an usher into the unknown, "one of those class of rovers you sometimes meet at sea, who never reveal their origin, never allude to home, and go rambling over the world as if pursued by some mysterious fate they cannot possibly elude." Byronic Toby seems an abstraction of the romantic spirit, dark complexioned, with "jetty locks" and "large black eyes," and a temperament to match: "He was a strange wayward being, moody, fitful, and melancholy—at times almost morose" (p. 32). He is an intense version of Tommo's own impulsiveness.

The deserting sailors are hardly ashore before they discover the folly of their plan. Instead of "broad and capacious valleys" beyond the first ridge, they find only mountains and ravines, and the breadfruit trees which were to supply them with food are nowhere in sight. Following what promises to be a native path, they are led by nightfall into a cul-de-sac, a dark chasm dripping with spray from a waterfall. Forced to sleep in this miserable hole, they are reduced from romantic expectations to a "dismal sense of our forlorn condition," and Tommo is nearly "unmanned" by his wretchedness (p. 46). Soaked to the skin, shivering and half-starved, the runaways cross over the dark territory through which the voyager must pass before he can gain the enchanted terrain beyond. The next morning, still undaunted by nature's inhospitality, the sailors catch their first sight of the interior valley, a vision of immaculate repose compared by Tommo to "the enchanted gardens in the fairy tale" (p. 49).

But, like the forbidding mountains which surround it, the beautiful valley is ironic ground. Tommo is soon to discover cryptic monuments which the natives cannot explain—natives who are silent about the ultimate fate of their cherished guest and whose spokesman is the mute Mehevi, grim equivalent of the mysterious monuments. And yet much delight awaits him as well, in the form of Fayaway and her happy friends. Surrounded by mystery and beauty, Tommo often feels "transported to some fairy region, so unreal did everything appear" (p. 134). And like the prisoner of fairies, he is never quite sure whether he is in paradise or hell. At times, indeed, he feels like an ass.

The moment he has caught his first "glimpse of the gardens of Paradise," Tommo begins to feel the torments of the damned. In Melville's mythology, penetration into nature's mysteries is often rewarded by a mutilating shock, and Tommo's first peep into the Typee valley is accompanied by the painful swelling of his leg which will cripple him throughout the remainder of his stay on the island. Significantly, he attributes the injury to the bite of a snake, "the congenial inhabitant of the chasm" where he and Toby spent the night. For the chasm and the valley are two halves of a whole, representative of the duality of the natural world which the wandering sailors have invaded.

As the island contains both the dark chasm and the sunny valley, so the valley contains spheres of love and fear. Though captivated by the simple life and physical beauty of the inhabitants, Tommo can never completely relax for long among them, and Toby's mysterious disappearance, along with his discovery of the grisly banquet in the warriors' hall, eventually overrules any delight he may have experienced with Fayaway. In time it is the paradisiacal green land which must be abandoned, while the open sea stands for freedom: "Oh glorious sight and sound of ocean! with what rapture did I hail you as familiar friends!" (p. 248). With Tommo's return to the sea his linear invasion of mystery becomes a circle, the dominant dimension of Melville's ironic diagram.

III

The movement of the narrative up to Tommo's entrance into the Typee valley is relatively straightforward and rapid. The quest here is simple and the obstacles obvious. But once Tommo is among the Typees, the movement of the story becomes serpentine and slow, defined both by his inability to decipher many of the mysterious events he encounters and by his wavering between acceptance of the savages' happy-go-lucky existence and his fear of their cannibalism and treachery. Instead of moving across mountains and ravines, he wanders haphazardly about the village and valley, making a series of discoveries—both pleasant and fearsome—which lead up to his eventual uncovering of the human remains in the banquet hall. At that point, the tensions of the preceding episodes are resolved, and the narrative line becomes once again simple and uncomplicated by uncertainties. Having received a positive answer to the question of the Typees' cannibalism, Tommo is glad to flee their paradise.

This section of the book, in which the quest pattern is at once complex and muted, looks forward to Melville's later writings—in particular his short stories, where the wanderings of the quester are limited and where the ironic landscape is restricted to a law office, a New England mountainside, or the decks of a Mississippi steamboat. The situation in the Typee Valley, moreover, is an anticipatory echo of "Benito Cereno," where we have once again a white man moving at great risk among savages, another white man held prisoner by the same savages, and an apparent valet who is actually a jailer. Like Tommo, Captain Delano vacillates between assurance and fear, and whereas the later story is made more complex by misdirecting the captain's suspicions towards the Spaniards, the real threat in both stories is concealed by the purposefully ambiguous demeanor of the savages. In both stories, too, we have a static pattern of action whose tension is caused by suspense and an atmosphere of threat, tension which ultimately explodes in violent, revelatory movement.

Because of the hidden "truth" of the situation in "Benito Cereno," the innocent, optimistic Captain Delano is often the unwitting victim of irony. What he sees as loving, dutiful kindness on the part of Babo, Cereno's former slave but now his master, is in reality a species of slow torture. The lock and key with which the Spaniard holds the giant mutineer, Atufal, "prisoner" is actually an emblem of his own captivity. The obedient attentiveness with which the "slaves" aid the Spaniards in carrying out menial tasks is actually the means by which a close watch is kept on the white prisoners. Certain contradictions to normal order and routine arouse Delano's suspicions, but because of his obtuseness he is unable to discover the truth.

Similar ironies appear in *Typee.* It is some time before Tommo discovers that Kory-Kory's attentiveness is a means of keeping watch on him, and in the interval he continues to marvel at the excellent care given him by the savages, particularly their insistence that he eat at every opportunity. Especially sardonic in this regard are Tommo's enthusiastic descriptions of the banquets in the Ti, for it is here that he eventually discovers the evidence which qualifies his earlier assertion, "it did my heart, as well as my body, good to visit it" (pp. 151–52). Amplifying this irony are a series of pig-man ambiguities, commencing with Toby's gloomy suspicion that the first dish of meat they are served is "baked baby" when it is actually a "juvenile porker" and ending with Tommo's discovery of what Kory-Kory hastens to explain away as "puarkee." To the natives, humans are known familiarly as "long pig," and Tommo's description of the hog butchery which precedes the "Feast of the Calabashes" is grimly (albeit innocently) suggestive: "Again and again he missed his writhing and struggling victim, but though puffing and panting with his exertions, he still continued them; and after striking a sufficient number of blows to have demolished an entire drove of oxen, with one crashing stroke he laid him dead at his feet" (p. 158). By omitting the word "pig" throughout the episode, Melville creates an ambiguity which Tommo does not grasp.

Equivocal devices like these keep the reader reminded of the possibility that the Typees are cannibals and that Tommo is intended for some ritual feast. At the same time, we are not sure until the final revelation that they *are* cannibals, and we never do find out whether Tommo is really being fattened for the kill or is merely the happy victim of the savages' proverbial hospitality. As in "Benito Cereno," moreover, the ambiguity seems to have a purpose beyond the creation of suspense. In the later story, Delano is kept from the truth by his stereotyped attitude towards Negroes, whom he regards as docile and unaspiring servants, and Spaniards, whom he associates with pirates and treachery. In *Typee,* Melville addresses himself to the tendency of his contemporaries either to regard the South Sea islanders as unregenerate cannibals all or to dismiss the idea of their cannibalism as perfectly ridiculous. Up until Tommo's final discovery, the Typees' cannibalism is merely a rumor, and the runaway sailor balances his fears by rhapsodic descriptions of their idyllic life. "Truth," declares Tommo, "loves to be centrally located, [and] is again found between the two extremes; for cannibalism to a certain moderate

extent is practised among several of the primitive tribes in the
Pacific, but it is upon the bodies of slain enemies alone; and
horrible and fearful as the custom is, immeasurably as it is to be
abhorred and condemned, still I assert that those who indulge in it
are in other respects humane and virtuous" (p. 205). Since
Melville is trying to establish this median "Truth," it is necessary
that his narrator witness the remains of a cannibal banquet
enjoyed by savages who are "in other respects humane and
virtuous."

Tommo, as an instrument of Truth, may be considered a
balancewheel of opinion, vacillating between the extreme positions maintained by society until his discovery of the cannibal
banquet provides him with definitive knowledge of the savages'
best and worst faults. At times he is Rousseauistic in his admiration of the Typees' nobility and peace of mind, their perpetual
hilarity and joyous good nature; at others, he trembles with fear
over the savages' well-known propensity for sudden treachery. As
long as his attention is on the fair aspects of the natives, Tommo is
able to maintain a Delano-like composure, but once he recalls the
proverbial fickleness of primitive man, fearful apprehensions seize
him. It is this vacillation between extreme attitudes which produces in *Typee* an equivalent of the symposium-circle found in
Melville's later works—a wholeness of opposite viewpoints. In
effect, *Typee* is an anatomy of savagery, a savagery which is
shown to be humane and treacherous, virtuous and cruel.

IV

Each character in the cast of primitive types that Tommo encounters in the Typee Valley represents one aspect of "natural"
man, often corresponding to the various ideas of savagery held by
Melville's contemporaries. Mehevi, chief of the Typees, corresponds to Rousseau's Noble Savage, a "splendid islander" with an
apollonian physique. Tommo calls him "Nature's nobleman" and,
while standing in awe of him, praises his hospitality. But Mehevi

has other characteristics as well, an "inflexible rigidity of expression" made even more terrible by his habitual silence (p. 119). It
is Mehevi's stern silence, especially, which dampens Tommo's
enjoyment of the "mirth, fun, and high good humor" reigning in
the valley. Whenever Mehevi appears, Tommo's "elasticity of
mind which [had] placed me beyond the reach of . . . dismal
forebodings" snaps back to "frightful apprehensions with regard to
my own fate" (pp. 123, 140).

Grim and silent, a Greek god in appearance, hospitable and
gracious, Mehevi is central to the mystery of the Typees. Ranged
about him are the other savage types: Mow-Mow, the brutal,
scarred, "ignoble" savage; Fayaway, who seems a cross between
Atala and Undine, an idealized Belle Sauvage; and the kindly
Kory-Kory, Tommo's man Friday and jailer. Domestic life is repre-
sented by Marheyo, a fatherly type who is the sailor's commiserating host, and his wife, Tinor, a model of primitive housewifery.
The valley is a microcosmic arrangement of alternatives, providing
a circular diagram of contrasts and designed to demonstrate that
primitive man is not one, easily categorized, type. Moreover, this
variety of savage types suggests yet another implication. As natural
men, the natives serve as correlatives of nature's plenitude, their
character types and range of moods an index to the "all" that was
for Melville a blank canvas of possibilities.

Kory-Kory is covered with tattoos, "representations of birds and
fishes, and a variety of most unaccountable-looking creatures,
suggesting to me the idea of a pictorial museum of natural history"
(p. 83). He is a savage Everyman and a correlative of the natural
world into which Tommo has crept and crawled, and as the fact of
his tattooing is a token of his savagery (Tommo shrinks with
disgust from the idea of having his own civilized hide marked
up), so the images presented on his body suggest his oneness with
nature. Similarly, the noble Mehevi is tattooed with a triangle, a
"sort of freemason's badge" which suggests to Tommo his "exalted
rank" as one of "Nature's noblemen" (pp. 228, 78), and the

ignoble Mow-Mow is decorated with an ugly scar, token of his
warlike nature.

It is Mow-Mow, not Mehevi, who attempts to kill Tommo
during his pell-mell escape from the valley, for, like Babo in
"Benito Cereno," he represents the dark malignity of natural
savagery. When the furiously swimming Mohawk-Marquesan
closes on his whaleboat, Tommo thrusts a boat hook at him, and
then—shocked by the "ferocious expression" on the savage's face—
faints dead away. The action anticipates the scene in "Benito
Cereno" where the "lividly vindictive" features of Babo, as he
writhes "snakishly" in an attempt to stab his former master, cause
the Spaniard to fall back in a dead faint. In both instances we are
given a glimpse of naked nature, embodied in the pure malevolence of which natural man is capable, a human coefficient of
Moby Dick's "two long crooked rows of white, glistening teeth,
floating up from the undiscoverable bottom . . . his vast,
shadowed bulk still half blending with the blue of the sea"
(p. 540).

The symbolic intimation of this disembodied grin—the merging
of the Whale with the natural element—is undeniable, and
symbolic too is Babo's "snakish writhing." But Mow-Mow's attack
is symbolic only to the extent that it represents the ferocity of
which natural man is capable. He is as symbolic as one of Cooper's
Indians, but no more. He is *of* nature, but is not Nature, for the
episode lacks the associational machinery of Melville's later works,
the imagery by which the Whale becomes personified natural
malevolence, or Babo the human counterpart of a poisonous
reptile.

By means of diagram and half-realized symbol, Melville seems
to be suggesting that the Typees, like Moby Dick, are animated
nature—a phenomenological whole that baffles inquiry. But these
patterns of intimation can be detected only by comparing them to
the later works. The materials of symbolism and irony are present,
and the young author seems to be hinting at their full significance,
but nothing comes of it. The patterns of appearance and reality,

sea and shore, enchantment and silence, delight and fear, all have symbolic counterparts in Melville's later work but are in themselves without the power of symbols. The microcosmic village, the relativistic range of savage types, the identification of primitive man with the natural world—all have their equivalents in the later work, but in *Typee* they remain latent, unrealized as symbolic potential.

When a contemporary of Melville's described *Typee* as "*Rasselas* rewritten by Irving," he wrote more wisely than he knew. For despite the book's ebullient, happy-go-lucky tone, its structure implies an underlying pessimism. Like *Rasselas*, *Typee* is a futile quest. The Irvingesque style might be compared to an ironic mask, like laughing Ishmael, whose jolliness is mockery, but if it was conceived as such, it plainly does not work. Perhaps the problem resulted from a conflict in purpose, for Melville seems to have been divided between a desire to report how things "really" were in the Islands and an equally strong desire to create a fiction, a planned series of clues, indirections, and climaxes, ironically conceived and executed. The "uses" of the hero-narrator are consequently at odds. At one moment we are to credit him with exposing civilized abuses against the hapless natives, at another we are to regard him as an unsuspecting dupe of cannibal tricks.

However it may have been, the voice which Melville chose for *Typee* is an insufficient instrument. It is the discursive voice of exposition, a fashionable manner that is fine for a travel book but too inflexible for the presentation of romantic ironies. Moreover, the first-person voice, dictated in his early works by autobiographical necessity (and the market), was often to give Melville trouble. Because of the frequent tension between his private artistic and philosophical aims and the need to satisfy his readers, who wished for more scenery and less skepticism, the first-person voice often betrayed him, leading him from the popular dimension towards the private sector of philosophic speculation. "I" is never in Melville's novels a consistently ironic mask, whether it be the "I" of Ishmael or Ahab.

It is notable, then, that in a number of his short stories Melville was able to establish a surprisingly consistent persona. Perhaps because of the very shortness of the form, he was able to keep his materials under better control than in his longer fiction, those risky voyages where he was apt to be caught by "a blast resistless" and blown far off course. Certainly the best of his short stories in this regard is "Bartleby," but the short sketch which served as an introduction to a volume of his collected stories, *Piazza Tales*, perhaps better suits the present purpose. Not only is the narrator a quester after mystery, but the imagery and situation recall both the "Fragment" and *Typee*. By examining it, we can see materials which appear in the early work integrated into an example of Melville's mature craft.

V

In "The Piazza," a landlocked sailor catches sight of a gleam on a mountaintop from the comfort of his piazza. His curiosity aroused, he "launches" his "yawl" (sets out on horseback) along a mountain road towards the distant gleam, hoping to find "the queen of fairies." Instead he finds a wretched mountain girl who lives in a miserable shack. Her only joy is dreaming about the "King Charming" who lives in the "white palace" below—the sailor's white-painted farmhouse. Disillusioned, the voyager returns to his piazza and contents himself thereafter with the theater of appearances. Commencing with a Spenserian motif, the sketch ends on a quixotic note—the suspension of disbelief for the sake of such pleasure as it may bring.

"The Piazza" somewhat resembles the early "Fragment," particularly in its use of a wildwood journey, but *Typee* is also evoked. Not only is the piazza compared to a ship, but the sailor dresses for his summertime voyage in "relics of my tropic sea-going" and compares the shy Marianna to "some Tahiti girl, secreted for a sacrifice, first catching sight, through palms, of Captain Cook." In the place of a violent climax, however, the ending of the story is peaceful, acquiescent, a pose which tends to dominate Melville's later work. The round trip here seems to imply harmonious accord with nature, or at least the wisdom of Candide, for the attitude of the returned sailor is one of calm acceptance.

But narrative attitude is a treacherous guide, and the sailor of "The Piazza" can be trusted no more than the sailor of *Moby-Dick.* The meaning of the story emerges from its structure, again a futile quest, and from the pattern of images and allusions with which [Melville builds up his ironic terrain, the landscape of deceptive scenery through which the quester passes unaware. The playing-off of this scenery against the attitude of the quester provides a paradoxical equivalent of the futile quest, and, by revealing the quester's essential blandness, in some ways qualifies his final attitude. It is the character of the quester, viewed against the ironic scenery, which supplies Melville's meaning, rather than the attitude of the quester alone.]

From the outset of the sketch, "The Piazza" contains a number of images and allusions which hint at the futile implications of the narrator's quest. The countryside around the piazza, for example, is described as "a very paradise of painters," a phrase suggesting the artificiality of the territory through which the sailor must travel. The illusoriness of the terrain is indicated by the view from the piazza, for "the circle of the stars [is] cut by the circle of the mountains. At least, so looks it from the house; though, once upon the mountains, no circle of them can you see. Had the site been chosen five rods off, this charmed ring would not have been." Another forbidding motif is supplied by implicit suggestions of danger and threat. The farmhouse is perched upon "a long land-slide of sleeping meadow, sloping away off from my poppy bed," a landscape implying disaster and narcotic slumber. The site of the house was wrested from "the Trogdolytes of those subterranean parts" and located where Orion (the blind quester) "flashed down his Damocles' sword" (a token of impending doom) and commanded "Build there."

Forbidding also are the conditions under which the gleam is first seen on the mountain. An "uncertain object," it is snuggled among a range of mountains whose perspective baffles and is "so situated as to be only visible, and then but vaguely, under certain conditions of light and shadow." When first sighted, the gleam is detected through the haze of a "wizard afternoon in autumn," when the woods, "having lost their first vermilion tint, dully smoked, like smouldering towns, when flames expire upon their prey." The sky is compared to a witches' cauldron, and "two sportsmen, crossing a red stubble buck-wheat field, seemed guilty Macbeth and foreboding Banquo." But these threatening portents mean nothing to the narrator. Viewing the "one spot of radiance, where all else was shade," he can only conclude that it marks "some haunted ring where fairies dance."

The contrast between the threatening landscape and the narrator's benign belief in fairies provides the main tension of the sketch, broken with his discovery of the pauper maiden. Much of the language, along with the quest, is borrowed explicitly from Spenser, cited by the sailor as his only guide to fairyland, which "must be voyaged to, and with faith." But the sailor's attitude towards the ambivalent, enchanted landscape is patently Quixote's, and he prizes the knight as "that sagest sage that ever lived." The sailor puts his faith in the good signs, such as the golden promise of a rainbow, and ignores the bad. The memory of his view from the piazza on an August noon, when the "vastness and the lonesomeness are so oceanic, and the silence and the sameness, too, that the first peep of a strange house, rising beyond the trees, is for all the world like spying, on the Barbary coast, an unknown sail," turns his thoughts not to the pirates one would normally associate with such a sail but to "my inland voyage to fairyland." No Ishmael, certainly, and near cousin to the benign Captain Delano, the landlocked sailor is the antithesis of Ahab, as persistently optimistic as the other is pessimistic. Throughout his journey, his enthusiasm is not at all lessened by the ominous signs which he encounters, like a "hanging orchard" which drops "Eve's apples," or "seek-no-furthers," or brambles that try to hold him back: "Fairy-land not yet, thought I, though the morning is here before me."

Like the landscape through which the sailor passes, the clearing in which he finds the object of his search is emblematic. The little, gray-colored cottage on the mountaintop seems at the very center of nature: "No fence was seen, no inclosure. Near by—ferns, ferns, ferns; further—woods, woods, woods; beyond—mountains, mountains, mountains; then—sky, sky, sky. Turned out in aerial commons, pasture for the mountain moon. Nature, and but nature, the house and all." Center of everything, center of nothing, the cottage is "set down on the summit, in a pass between the two worlds, participant of neither," and its centrality is symbolized by its roof, one half of which is shiny with new shingles, the other weather-stained and mossy. This pairing of lights and darks, like the two halves of the tortoise in "The Encantadas," or the chasm and the valley in *Typee*, suggests the balance of opposing forces that is nature for Melville.

A similar balance informs the conclusion of the sketch. Although the narrator decides to stick to his piazza, to accept nature as a theater of illusion, "every night, when the curtain falls, truth comes in with darkness. No light shows from the mountain." Fairyland is the gift of sunlight; darkness, in dimming the golden window, brings back thoughts of "the weary face behind it." Despite the sailor's continued faith in sunlight, once it is removed he is "haunted by Marianna's face, and many as real a story." It is the realization of the truth of darkness that gives point to the sailor's tale, for it is the same truth which has revealed itself in imagery and allusion throughout the narrative, hinting of the blackness that underlies nature's bright gildings. But there is no sign that the sailor even now understands the implication of those signs, or the meaning of the Chinese creeper which climbs the post of his piazza, a "starry bloom" containing "millions of strange, cankerous worms, which, feeding upon those blossoms, so shared their blessed hue, as to make it unblessed evermore."

The shock of absolute darkness only temporarily awakens him to reality, the misery concealed by sunny reflections. Like Captain Delano, he has passed through his experience relatively unscathed and is not responsible for the dark implications of imagery and allusion. It is Melville alone who constructs the maze by which his questers are ultimately baffled, however much he may sympathize with their heroism. As early as the "Fragment from a Writing Desk," we can see him experimenting with the indirect use of images, and though their appearance in *Typee* suggests a purposeful ambivalence, it is only in his "pure" fiction, commencing with *Mardi,* that we begin to detect patterns of ironic complexity which point towards the paradoxical textures of *Moby-Dick,* "Benito Cereno," *The Confidence-Man,* and *Billy Budd.* In these later works, as in "The Piazza," Melville employs point of view, whether first or third person, as a medium of indirection, voicing attitudes more or less consistently undercut by the implication of imagery.

Employed usually to qualify the absolute implications of the quest, Melville's ironic images and allusions are an important element of the ambivalent terrain through which his questers voyage and may be regarded as a persistent reminder of the dangers of imperfect perception. Though Melville's style may vary, changing from the baroque excesses of *Moby-Dick* to the neoclassical balance of *The Confidence-Man,* and though the material of his narratives may change from Ahab's heroic whale hunt to the confidence man's pursuit of confidence, the ironic use of imagery and the structure of the futile quest are intrinsic to his art throughout. Inseparable, they provide the detailed dimensions of his ironic diagram.

Chapter Three

Mardi: A Chartless Voyage,
But Not Without a Plan

Written to benefit from the critical praise of *Typee, Omoo* has all the liabilities of a sequel. Perhaps the most light-hearted of Melville's novels, it is also the most formless—a picaresque ramble which lacks the structural elements associated with his other works. "Omoo" means "wanderer," and the narrator is exactly that, wandering over the islands with a prototype picaro—Doctor Long Ghost—for a companion. If there is a quest, it is the generalized motive of the tourist, not the infatuated search of the romantic quester. But in *Mardi,* the basic form once again is the romantic quest, quixotically conceived. As in *Typee,* the narrator is a sailor who has become bored with shipboard life and who deserts with a companion for the far distance. By means of a series of symbolic thresholds, he passes from the "real" world into the fanciful realm of Mardi, a journey which commences as an adventurous trip to the Kingsmill Islands but which is blown off course by a "blast resistless" generated by Melville's discovery of Rabelais, Robert Burton, and Sir Thomas Browne. A chartless voyage through the world of the mind, *Mardi* moves from a mood of ennui to one of great physical excitement, and from there to a purely speculative mood with an emphasis on philosophical dialogue, satire, and fantasy.

Instrumental in promoting the many changes of mood and

mode in *Mardi* is the "voice" of the narrator. At first the voice is a strong, first-person presence reminiscent of Tommo, but as the story moves into the fanciful realm it becomes a disembodied, disinterested presence who, adopting the third-person point of view, attends the voyagers in Media's canoe. At the outset, this narrating voice suggests a personality constructed of contrasts: good-natured yet strong-willed; affectionate yet often sarcastic; earnest yet facetious; observant, impressionable, enthusiastic, and intelligently prejudiced. Self-contradictory, Taji is the embodiment of the romantic ego, his very contradictoriness preparing the way for the opening diagram of opposed points of view which characterizes the Mardian tour.

Like Ishmael (whom he resembles), the rhapsodic persona who dominates the first part of *Mardi* is the vital spirit necessary to the romantic quest. Outward, with or without charts, escaping monotony and stagnation, Melville's questers move, and the narrator of these opening chapters is predictably impulsive, visionary, a man of flesh who is in danger of being invaded by his soul: "I cast my eyes downward to the brown planks of the dull, plodding ship, silent from stem to stern; then abroad. In the distance, what visions were spread!" (p. 7). A transcendental version of Tommo, the deserting sailor is full of an egoistical vitality: viewing a flight of birds, he supposes "my spirit must have sailed in with it; for directly, as in a trance, came upon me the cadence of mild billows laving a beach of shells, the waving of boughs, and the voices of maidens, and the lulled beatings of my own dissolved heart, all blended together" (p. 8). This is the voice both of Tommo, beguiled by "olden voyagers," and of the dreaming masthead philosopher who is apt to take disastrous tumbles into the All. He contains the quixotic impulse that makes his final nihilism possible.

Like Tommo, the narrator of *Mardi* is exposed to the various aspects of nature: the horror of dead calms, the hateful microcosm of the shark world, the psychological bruising of isolation in an immensity of ocean waste. Throughout, however, he remains optimistic, transcendental: "Now hate is a thankless thing. So let us only hate hatred; and once give love play, we will fall in love with a unicorn. Ah! the easiest way is the best; and to hate, a man must work hard" (p. 41). The cruel indifference of the ocean is gilded over—"Oh, Ocean, when thou choosest to smile, more beautiful thou art than flowery mead or plain!" (p. 50)—and the voice lapses into folly as blind as Captain Delano's admiration of naked nature: "As well hate a seraph as a shark. Both were made by the same hand. And that sharks are lovable, witness their domestic endearments. No Fury so ferocious, as not to have some amiable side" (p. 40).

There is surely something here of the man who can bed down with savages, who is willing to come to terms with any horror, be it animal or human. But the narrator of *Mardi* lacks Ishmael's saving skepticism. For him, "All things form but one whole," a benevolent globe resting in the hand of God. "In a theocracy, what is to fear?" (p. 12). There is no mention of Solomon's wisdom, no hint of invisible spheres, of the blackness of darkness. That is to be the part of Babbalanja, for until the shock of Taji's discovery that Yillah is dead, the narrator manages to maintain throughout an air of optimism and philanthropy.

Even before Babbalanja appears, however, there are hints that the narrator's point of view is to be taken ironically. The strongest of these is the character of his companion, Jarl, the "Skyeman." On one level Jarl is a symbolic accouterment, like Toby and Queequeg, a saga figure, descendant of the Viking questers. Blond, taciturn, Nordic, he is knowledgeable in the ways of the sea and an ideal companion for the questing narrator. He is also a type of squire, who knows his place and never questions the captaincy of the little vessel. He does the work, while the narrator sits "in the boat's quiet stern, steering and philosophizing at one time and the same" (p. 44). In his capacity of squire, however, Jarl is something of a Sancho Panza. When it is first proposed that the two sailors desert the *Arcturion*, Jarl "bluntly" declares "that the scheme was a crazy one; he had known of such a thing but thrice before; and in every case the runaways had never afterwards been heard of." But in the end, "seeing my resolution immovable, he bluntly swore that he would follow me through thick and thin" (p. 17).

The contrast between the narrator's mystical adventurousness and Jarl's commonsensical, if often superstitious, misgivings, eventually opens into a more complex arrangement: the combination of king, historian, philospher, and poet that sets sail with Taji in pursuit of the missing Yillah, and the means by which the complex personality of the narrator is anatomized into a polysensuum, a spectrum of contrasting attitudes. Narrative dialogue hardens into a philosophic symposium, and the originally open impulse of the narrator is narrowed to a single-minded desire to find the missing Yillah—only one of several attitudes. The voice of narration ceases to be a simple, ironic vehicle and becomes elevated to the position of an omniscient author, a third-person point of view which regards Taji as merely another identity, one voice among the others aboard Media's canoe. And yet all of the participants in the sea-borne symposium are but constituents of a larger subjective consciousness—the chartless voyager.

This structure of expanding contrasts provides *Mardi* with an artful if confusing series of foliations. From the fatuous optimism of the early narrator, which is balanced by the truculent doubts of Jarl, to the wide range of viewpoints aboard Media's canoe and on the islands it touches, to the final, suicidal farewell of the last chapter, Melville presents a diagram of alternatives, qualifying the defiant absolutism of his quester by the terms of the quest itself.

II

Melville's questers approach the heart of mystery by a series of thresholds, and the movement from the phenomenal world of the outset of *Mardi* to the noumenal realm of the archipelago is marked by a series of increasingly fantastical episodes. The progression ends with Chapter 38, "The Sea on Fire," in which the voyagers are surrounded by a phosphorescent sea of "pallid white," a phenomenon which can be scientifically explained but which inspires superstitious misgivings. It is this incident of natural magic which is the final threshold into mystery, for the next episode is the discovery of the raft of Aleema and beautiful Yillah. Until Taji's encounter with the raft, his world has been literally "phenomenal," an environment of maddening calms and disastrous storms. But having passed through the eerie sea of fire, as through a door into fairyland, he enters a region of imagination, peopled by creatures of fancy.

The marvelous sea of fire, Taji explains, is caused by the glow generated by "myriads of microscopic mollusca," which have their counterpart in the terrestrial firefly. The glow of the firefly, notes Taji, is "a beacon to love," but the glow of the "fire-fish" leads to its destruction, for their radiance "reveals them to their foes." Foreboding characteristics such as this are typical of Melville's many thresholds, suggesting the inadvisability of the quest into mystery. Aside from the dreadful calms and even more dreadful sea beasts earlier encountered by the adventurers, perhaps the most ominous of the thresholds crossed by Taji and Jarl is the derelict trading brigantine, *Parki*, where they encounter the outlandish Samoa and Annatoo.

The *Parki* is a sort of floating wildwood, "miserably cobbled together with planks of native wood, and fragments of a wreck," with "unpainted sides . . . of a dark-colored, heathenish-looking wood" and a tiller made from "a wry-necked, elbowed bough" that thrusts "itself through the deck, as if the tree itself was fast rooted in the hold" (pp. 68, 65). These bizarre, symbolic furnishings link the *Parki* with the equally uncouth *Pequod*. Whereas the *Pequod* is named after an Indian tribe, the *Parki* bears the name of "a high chief, the tallest and goodliest looking gentleman in all the Sandwich Islands" (p. 68). But the word also suggests Mungo Park, that explorer into the heart of darkness whose name always connoted for Melville the encounter of civilization and savagery.

That encounter in Melville's fiction is often a harbinger of disaster. The *Pequod*, manned by a barbaric crew and a Sioux-like captain, is sunk by Moby Dick, and the *San Dominick*, with its crew of Ashantees and Spaniards, is the scene of a bloody mutiny. The *Parki*, which set sail with "a mixed European and native crew, about thirty in number," is attacked by "Cholos, or half-breed Spaniards, from the Main; one half Spanish, the other half quartered between the wild Indian and the devil" (p. 69), and the massacre-haunted hull—itself a mixture of civilized planks and native wood—has not long to live.

"Murder," remarks Taji, "is catching" (p. 115), and nine days after abandoning the *Parki*, he commits the act which links him to Cain. On the dawn of that day, having passed through the ominous sea of fire, the voyagers discover a noddy asleep on the peak of their sail: "Its plumage was snow-white, its bill and legs blood-red," and when the sail of Aleema's raft is later sighted, "It looked like one of many birds; for half intercepting our view, fell showers of plumage: a flight of milk-white noddies flying downward to the sea" (p. 126). In "Benito Cereno" the noddy makes a symbolic appearance as a bird "so called from its lethargic, somnambulistic character, being frequently caught by hand at sea," a coefficient of Captain Delano—also white, also somnambulistic—but here it has a different, if equally ominous, significance. The whiteness of mystery mingles with the color of blood, all pointing the way to the raft, where Taji will discover the miraculously pale Yillah and will murder Aleema.

Like the forehead of Moby Dick, the brow of the old priest is "deep-graven in wrinkles," containing characters "which no Champollion nor gypsy could have deciphered. He looked old as the elderly hills; eyes sunken, though bright; and head white as the summit of Mount Blanc" (p. 130). This Chaldean figure stands guard before a tent whose mystery the questing Taji, afire with curiosity and ignoring all warnings and omens, yearns to penetrate. The tent produces Yillah, ending the episode but initiating the marvelous events which are to follow. The murder of the priest, at once unpremeditated and unwarranted, casts a shadow on Taji's bliss with Yillah, who soon disappears, occasioning the second phase of the journey. By killing Aleema, Taji has separated himself "from himself" and has exchanged the restlessness of the wanderer for a more demonic unrest. Henceforth his adventure is haunted by the past, and as he pursues Yillah, so he is pursued in turn by the vengeful sons of Aleema. Taji's freedom seems absolute, but he is caught between the forces of his desire for some unattainable ideal and the consequences of his past act. By that act, therefore, he seems to damn himself to failure from the very first.

Haunted by guilt, possessed by desire for the absolute, Taji sets sail into a territory which seems an endless realm of possibilities but which proves, in the end, the roundness of a finite zero. The contrast between his yearning and the relativism of the terrain through which he passes in his search provides the controlling irony of the many ancillary paradoxes with which *Mardi* is constructed. But the symbolism of the opening chapters has already suggested that the quest is doomed to failure, that it can only end in the nihilism of "Mardi behind: an Ocean before." Traveling the complete circuit of the archipelago in search of Yillah, the unattainable ideal which the Faustian man is committed to pursue, Taji is predictably unsuccessful. In the end he sets sail for "the deep beyond," the unknown world beyond the terrestrial reef. Willing himself an "unreturning wanderer," Taji strikes a Byronic pose before plunging into the "realm of shades," the inevitable death that awaits the man who breaks through the circle of life.

III

Circle and line are infinitely expandable. The number of islands that Taji and his companions visit are limited only by the author's inventiveness and his readers' patience (in *Mardi* the first exceeds the last), and this infinitude is perfectly suited to the roving romantic spirit. Still, though Taji is a projection of Melville's identity as a "seeker not a finder yet," though Melville, with Taji,

has "chartless voyaged," blown by a "blast resistless," the voyage
has been within his, not Taji's, consciousness. From the outset, by
means of ironic contrast, Melville reveals an imperfect sympathy
with his narrator's youthful idealism, and if Taji's quest for Yillah
mirrors Melville's own search for truth, so the round, relativistic
world of the archipelago and the skeptical implications of the
many dialogues among those who accompany Taji mirror the
uncertainties which plagued Melville's intellectual pursuit. Both
line and circle are projections of Melville's "mind-world," symbols
of his divided nature. If the line represents a voyage in the world
of the mind, so the circle represents the limits of inquiry. However much it may expand, it never breaks its baffling relativity.

Central to the meaning of the journey round the world-archi-
pelago is the island of Juam, encountered by the voyagers soon
after they start on their journey. Geographically a confirmation of
the island metaphor in *Typee*, Juam contains a hidden valley at its
center which can be reached only by a tunnel. Through darkness
into light move the pilgrims, a passage which would seem to imply
an absolute discovery, but the hidden valley, like the Whale
Circle in *Moby-Dick* or the Typee Valley, is a center of dubious
repose. It is sheltered from the raging ocean beyond, but the very
peace of the valley is accentuated by the audible booming of the
waves outside. Further ironic contrast is provided by the geog-
raphy of the place, for when the eastern half is lighted by the
afternoon sun, the western side is made gloomy by a somber
shadow. "Thus cut in twain by masses of day and night, it seemed
as if some Last Judgment has been enacted in the glen" (p. 217).
The valley is an emblem of the totality of existence, peacefulness
in the midst of turbulence, but a peacefulness which is itself
divided into darks and brights—like the two halves of the cottage
roof in "The Piazza."

The silence of the valley accentuates the pounding of the surf,
and the light part of its mystic chiaroscuro serves to bring into
sharper relief the profundity of its darknesses. Similarly, the
inhabitant king of the valley, Donjalolo, lives in indolence, which

makes his misery even more extreme. Though ruler of his people, he is held prisoner by their laws and may never leave the valley. An early version of Don Benito Cereno, another ruler-prisoner, Donjalolo is listless and enervate, the embodiment of decadence, but only because he is forbidden to be otherwise. His kingdom contains two villages, "one to the west, the other to the east," between which he is carried each day. Moving from east to west, with the sun, Donjalolo is a sun king who shuns the daylight, dwelling always (like Don Benito) in shadow, a figurative expression of "that Calvinistic sense of Innate Depravity and Original Sin." The incident which led to the traditional incarceration of the kings of Juam was a fratricide, the archetypal crime of brother against brother.

Symbolic also are the two dwellings of Donjalolo. His "House of Morning" is a fantastic mixture of artificial and natural elements, each an emblem of the male principle, the whole "raised upon a natural mound . . . almost completely filling up a deep recess between deep-green and projecting cliffs" (p. 231). Its contrasting counterpart, the "House of the Afternoon," is a natural grotto at the other end of the valley, from whose womblike interior springs a Wordsworthian stream of life. The grotto lies concealed in the fertile valley, the "still, panting glen of Willamilla, nested so close by the mountains, and a goodly green mark for the archer in the sun" (p. 234). But this womb is haunted by images of death, hints of ultimate darkness: the cataract within is a "sheeted ghost," and the vines that grow there, though green at their tops, are shriveled and tattered lower down.

The two houses in the valley provide a further series of contrasts, comparable to those in Melville's "The Paradise of Bachelors and the Tartarus of Maids." Here, as there, the opposition of mood and gender suggests the division between the male and female principles, the one gay and splendid, but essentially fruitless, the other fruitful but wretched. Still further division is indicated by the construction of the grotto and the grove, for the first is a natural "mansion," while the other is a product of artifice, a series of mazelike passages that leads to the inner "citadel." There lies Donjalolo at night, reclining Pharaoh-like and gazing heavenward "at the torch-light processions in the skies, when, in state, the suns march to be crowned" (p. 240). Though a sun king, Donjalolo is compared to a sarcophagus, for like the Bachelors of the Inner Temple, he is essentially dead. Surrounded by the luxurious machinery of copulation and frui-tion, he is without children and is literally as well as figuratively indivisible. Moving between the phallic House of the Morning and the womblike House of the Afternoon, the "insphered sphere" is the everything that is nothing, prisoner of the Omphalos.

His sloth, however, is enforced, and Donjalolo occasionally seeks to voyage vicariously, to learn about foreign lands through agents. But the witnesses, like the whaling authorities cited by Ishmael, predictably contradict each other, and their accounts only verify the multiplicity of worldly existence. Returning from the island of Rafona, they present conflicting accounts of that place, driving Donjalolo to cry out in despair, "How hard is truth to be come at by proxy." Dismissing his court, he retires, while Bab-balanja explains to the voyagers that both witnesses were wrong and both were right: "In various places [Rafona] is of various hues" (p. 250). Babbalanja is a version of Imlac, a master of the circular, skeptical view. Donjalolo is a type of Rasselas, but unlike Johnson's questing hero, he is kept forever from the experience of encounter with the puzzling contrasts of life.

It is Taji who pursues the phantom of happiness around the world. Disregarding the lesson of Juam's microcosmic world-circle, he sets forth in search of Yillah, the beautiful emblem of a blissful absolute. Like Ahab, who also perseveres in an impossible errand, he perishes. Skeptical Babbalanja, like skeptical Ishmael, survives, but as his conversion to the doctrines of Alma testifies, his skepti-cism (like Ishmael's) is not perfect. He succumbs to a belief that Melville was never able to espouse, but his earlier uncertainty and his eventual conversion are projections of Melville's own crosscur-rents of doubt and desire to believe: like Melville, he can "neither believe, nor be comfortable in his unbelief; and he is too honest and courageous not to try to do one or the other." Babbalanja does the "one," and although his conversion seems certainly to have been a synthetic epiphany, it is posed as an alternative to the life-in-death satanism chosen by Taji, one answer to the puzzle of Willamilla and the larger enigma of Mardi.

IV

The difference between the attitudes of Taji and Babbalanja provides the device by which Melville hoped to express his divided attitude towards the existential problem. Though Taji is the narrator, by means of soliloquy and dramatic dialogue Babbalanja is permitted to become a subjective identity, and since Taji becomes a shadowy presence during much of the voyage, it is the philosopher who eventually emerges as the chief voice of the book. This, in turn, necessitates a further dichotomy (like the insphered spheres of Willamilla), and Babbalanja is given two personalities. In the company of his fellow travelers, he maintains a jocular, protective mask and reveals his inner doubts only through soliloquy or the occasional escape of his devil, Azzageddi, through whose mad babblings he can express black doubts.

The drift of technique and point of view here, like the dichotomy of characterization, looks forward to *Moby-Dick,* where the personable Ishmael gives way to pessimistic Ahab, who is in turn qualified by the skeptical chapters on cetology and whaling. When Ishmael's person is replaced by the persona of the cetology chapters, Ahab—attended by the Azzageddi-like Pip—advances as the Babbalanja-like advocate of blackness. Immediately before Taji sheds all his illusions to become Ahab-like in his total commitment to darkness, Babbalanja undergoes a conversion akin to Ishmael's mystic experience around the whale tubs. It is by such means that Melville maintains a balance of attitudes which reflects the complexity of the perceived world.

Until his conversion, Babbalanja is secretive, cryptic, self-protective. Until *his* conversion, Taji is outgoing, rhapsodic, expressing himself in rodomontade: "Ay: many, many souls are in me. In my tropical calms, when my ship lies tranced on Eternity's main, speaking one at a time, then all with one voice: an orchestra of many French bugles and horns, rising, and falling, and swaying, in golden calls and responses" (p. 367). This is the voice of the transcendent ego, in which self and deity become one, the all-inclusive "I" that is "fixed and luminous forever in the foundationless firmament." And Taji's quest is an exercise in extroversion, attended by the dangers which await the masthead philosopher in *Moby-Dick*.

Babbalanja, conversely, is intent upon inner mysteries, "that which is beneath the seeming; the precious pearl within the shaggy oyster. I probe the circle's center; I seek to evolve the inscrutable" (p. 352). He is fascinated by the "world of wonders insphered within the spontaneous consciousness," the "mystery within the obvious, . . . obviousness within the mystery." The dangers which threaten him are those of the helmsman who stares too long into the fire, madness of despair tokened by his alter ego, Azzageddi. Ahab-like in his intensity, Babbalanja also resembles Ishmael in being the advocate of "deep thought whose language is laughter," and like Ishmael also, he has found that "we can not live without hearts; though the heartless live longest. Yet hug your hearts, ye handful that have them; 'tis a blessed inheritance" (pp. 613–14).

Two of the other voyagers, the historian, Mohi, and the poet, Yoomy, present a similar split of attitudes, and the keystone to all four is King Media. The voice of mediation, he expresses the Olympian balance of eighteenth-century skepticism, the Montaigne-based *"Que sçay-je?"* of a Johnson or a La Rochefoucauld: "Though in your dreams you may hie to the uttermost Orient, yet all the while you abide where you are" (p. 370). Apparently as fixed as a star, he regards philosophical inquiry as utterly futile, for man can have no "final, last thoughts." Even the wisest man, notes this wise man, is "ever unfixed," showing "tropical calm without" but containing "a thousand contrary currents" within (p. 370). Like many skeptics, Media tells us much about himself in speaking of others: he is among his fellow voyagers when they become converts to the doctrines of Alma.

With the swing of four of the pilgrims to absolute optimism, Taji is thrown into extreme nihilism and becomes once again a strong identity. Like Ahab, he becomes "the hunter that never rests! the hunter without a home!" Forswearing philanthropy, he hardens his heart against the world: "Hyenas filled me with their laughs; death-damps chilled my brow; I prayed not, but blasphemed" (p. 639). However implausible this Byronic transformation (no more unlikely, after all, than Media's sudden conversion or Babbalanja's epiphanic vision), it prepares the way for the melodramatic discovery of Yillah's ghost-corpse and Taji's Ahab-like resolution to "steer [my] own fate," to become "my own soul's emperor; and my first act is abdication!" (p. 654). Taji's sudden change seems to hint that extreme pessimism is not much different from extreme optimism, that—like Babbalanja's doubt and faith—they are easily exchanged.

In the final opposition of faith and denial, Melville seems to be expressing the dilemma of romanticism, defined by Babbitt as the difference between mere Byronic "restlessness" and the "divine discontent of religion." The one produces disillusionment and leads to realms of darkness and death; the other is a movement from turbulence into great inner calm. But religious contentment depends upon an acceptance of a transcendent truth, an absolute beyond the grasp of individual comprehension. Religious contentment is essentially a surrender of self, a sort of death-in-life, and the travelers who settle for the peace of Serenia can only do so by abandoning the (for Melville) imperative voyage out. Taji, in choosing to sail on, elects the romantic position of eternal restlessness, and if it can be demonstrated that his phantom of lost delight is pure illusion, so can it also be shown that Serenia, after all, is a Utopia, and no more of this earth than Yillah.

There yet remains a third choice, an alternative to the surrender of Babbalanja or the continuing, futile quest of Taji. Lombardo, Melville's fabulous artificer of the *Mardi*-like "Koztanza," by experiencing the chaos of the world through the creative act, undergoes a mystic experience akin to the vision which Babbalanja has in Serenia. Where Babbalanja is led upward, to an infinite point in heaven, Lombardo's progress is downward into himself. By writing his epic, he moved "deeper and deeper into himself; and like a resolute traveler, plunging through baffling woods, at last was rewarded for his toils." Moving inward, the artist discovers "a serene, sunny, ravishing region; full of sweet scents, singing birds, wild plaints, roguish laughs, prophetic voices" (p. 595). Born of woe ("Woe it is, that reveals these things"), the creative act can result in perfect happiness, the balanced contentment of having "created the creative." Deep within the most troubled soul, at the center of paired contraries, there may often be found the long-sought pastoral haven.

When he wrote *Mardi*, Melville was full of confidence in his artistic powers and was at the height of his public fame. The exuberant, unchanneled overflow of his creative spirit is all too evident in his first attempt at unbridled romance. The delight which Lombardo felt was undoubtedly shared by the author of *Mardi*. It was in a much different mood that Melville wrote *Pierre*, and in that book the authorial descent is rewarded not by bliss but by the same void of inner nonbeing that destroys Taji: "For the more and the more that he wrote, and the deeper and the deeper that he dived, Pierre saw the everlasting elusiveness of Truth; the universal lurking insincerity of even the greatest and purest written thoughts" (p. 399). Instead of discovering the hermaphroditic contentment of Lombardo, Pierre has a vision of Enceladus, the "repulsed . . . heaven assaulter," who, "despairing of any other mode of wreaking his immitigable hate, turned his vast trunk into a battering-ram, and hurled his own arched-out ribs again and again against the invulnerable steep" (p. 407). Always facetious in his presentation of the possibilities of transcendent bliss, as if mocking his own deep desire for it, Melville became less and less willing to present it as an alternative to the blackness of despair.

But even in his last works, there are blessed creatures like Nehemiah and Billy Budd, whose placidity feeds on an inner certainty, nonetheless real for being foolish. To the end Melville believed the Pythagorean axiom that each man discovers no more or less than that which he contains within himself, "the incomprehensible stranger," "mysterious indweller" of the soul: "In our hearts we fashion our own gods. . . . Ourselves are Fate" (*WJ,* pp. 320–21). This is "the meaning of that story of Narcissus, who because he could not grasp the tormenting, mild image he saw in the fountain, plunged into it and was drowned. But that same image, we ourselves see in all rivers and oceans. It is the image of the ungraspable phantom of life; and this is the key to it all." Pierre's authorial descent may be seen as an extension of his absolutist quest, darkened by discouragement into pessimism, and becoming at last, like Ahab's harpoon, a blasphemous instrument. It cannot, unlike Lombardo's all-inclusive, relativistic "Koztanza," lead him into repose.

Surrounded by plenitude, each of the questers in *Mardi* makes a choice—from the surrender of Babbalanja to the homeless hunt of Taji—and the nature of that choice is determined by the "indweller," the devout believer hidden within Babbalanja or the flint-hard pessimist obscured by Taji's superficial philanthropy. But no one choice cancels the possible validity of another, and in the final arrangement we are provided with a circle of relationships more or less reminiscent of the earlier ring of attitudes, a ring of metaphysical musical chairs in which the players have changed positions within an unchanging round. It is easy enough to detect Melville's predilection for certain attitudes, but his structural insistence upon reasonable alternatives, however factitiously mounted, is the basis even here for the puzzling ambiguities of his later masterpieces, the skillful dissembling of *Moby-Dick, The Confidence-Man, Clarel,* and *Billy Budd.*

Chapter Four

Redburn and White-Jacket:
The Structure of Initiation

Because of similar themes and settings, *Redburn* and *White-Jacket* may be considered two parts of a whole. The one, through the misadventures of a spoiled, lubberly boy during his first voyage as a deck hand on a merchantman, is concerned with youth's initial encounter with the world. The other, a much more complex work, uses an experienced sailor's first enlistment aboard a man-of-war as the occasion to structure a microcosm: the world of the warship is an allegorical equivalent of the real world. Both experiences are initiatory, and both books are concerned with the problem of the alien individual in a hostile environment.

Since the movement of each book is characterized by the ritualistic stages of initiation, the passage of innocence from station to station into experience, they both share with Melville's other works the linear aspect of his diagram. But each differs greatly from the other in the extent to which the line of initiatory advance dominates the narrative. In *Redburn,* particularly in the first two-thirds of the book, the story is limited to the innocent hero's education in the cruel ways of the world. But the continuity of White-Jacket's adventures aboard the *Neversink* is obscured by numerous digressions, encyclopedic discussions of various aspects of life aboard the world ship. These digressions correspond to the "circular" elements of *Mardi* and *Moby-Dick,* and, like the visits to the islands and the cetology chapters, they tend to balk the advance of the story proper. Indeed, strictly speaking there is no "story" in *White-Jacket*, no appreciable narrative thread. The book is primarily descriptive, a series of essays about life on a man-of-war which is held together by the tensions of that life as they bear upon the narrator, whose cumulative experience signifies the process of initiation.

The structure of *White-Jacket* bears careful study because of its obvious similarities to *Moby-Dick*, but *Redburn* should not be ignored because of its apparent simplicity. For one thing, the linear element closely corresponds to the quest pattern in *Typee* and *Mardi*: a young boy, early fascinated by tales of the sea and faraway places, is forced by circumstances to work as a deck hand, and his experiences aboard ship and in the slums of Liverpool provide a sharp contrast to his early illusions. This line of development is complicated by a second theme, Redburn's search for the England of his father's day, a quest in which he is ultimately frustrated. Further complexity emerges with the introduction of Harry Bolton, whose worldly wisdom is contrasted with Redburn's innocence, but who proves in the end to be entirely unadaptable to the seagoing life which Redburn has gradually accepted. It is the introduction of Harry Bolton into the narrative which emphasizes Redburn's development: significantly, the unadaptable Harry goes on, like all of Melville's absolute characters, to his death, while Redburn makes the return trip of the relativist.

Despite the implications of Redburn's round trip, the structure of the book is dominated by the linear dimension of Melville's ironic diagram. *White-Jacket*, by contrast, is primarily cyclical: the "quest," such as it is, consists chiefly of a rambling tour through the various levels and departments of the floating microcosm provided by a ship of the line. It is not farfetched to suggest that the important word in the subtitle of *Redburn* is "Voyage," in *White-Jacket*, "World." Much attention in *Redburn* is paid to the kinetic fact of motion—across the ocean, through Liverpool, and into the English countryside—the movement in *White-Jacket* is

planetary, enforced by the self-conscious imposition of the limitations necessitated by the central conceit of the "World in a Man-of-
War." We remember Redburn as generally being in motion:
climbing masts, washing out pigpens, wandering through Liverpool, trudging along a country road. But there are few episodes in
which White-Jacket *does* anything—the picture we retain is of the
narrator reclining in the rigging of the main-royal, listening to the
tales of his shipmates. Like Ishmael (after the *Pequod* leaves port),
he is a passive participant, who talks about others more than about
himself, and though the book is unified by the observant "I," it is
largely made up of anecdotes in which the narrator takes little or
no part. When he is involved in action it is usually as an unwilling victim—as when he is kicked out of his mess or hauled up for
a flogging or pitched from a yardarm into the sea. The situation,
promoted by the closed structure of the book, contrasts with the
bustle stirred up by that energetic tourist, Redburn.

Again, it is dangerous to draw simple conclusions about Herman Melville's "little nursery tale." The introduction of Harry
Bolton, along with the use of a complexly ironic viewpoint, makes
any hasty assumptions about the implications of its linear structure
foolish. Still, despite some qualifying variations, the theme of
Redburn depends upon the "before-after" sequence of maturation,
and the important contrast is the difference between innocence
and experience. The emphasis throughout is upon Redburn. In
White-Jacket, however, this emphasis is blurred by the many
digressions, episodes in which White-Jacket takes little or no part.
And yet there is a connection between the world ship and the
narrator, for the digressions bear upon the central issue (life
within a tightly organized, stratified society maintained by a
democratic government) and upon the problems of White-Jacket
as a member (and victim) of that society. Unlike Redburn, who
comes to tolerate and even participate in the sailor's world, White-
Jacket is initiated not into the man-of-war society but *out* of it,
and his stay aboard the *Neversink* is a purgatory which ends only
with his departure from the ship. Though early accepted by Jack

Chase, the aristocrat of the maintop, White-Jacket remains at odds with the crew and the system and does not at the end—unlike Redburn—seem to have been much changed by his ordeal, a fact which corresponds with the over-all stasis of the book.

The style of each story corresponds to its ironic burden. In *Redburn,* the narrative commences with a simple, facetious manner which points up the naïveté of the youth who has entertained such romantic notions about the sea and ships. As the boy matures the style becomes more complex, at last turning from an instrument of self-ridicule to rhetoric aimed against the poverty of Liverpool slums and the conditions aboard immigrant vessels bound for America, alternating with commiserating sympathy for the misfortunes of Redburn's companion, Harry. That is, as the boy changes, so does the style. In *White-Jacket* there is no such progression, but rather a series of styles, each adopted for a special occasion—jocular, sly, self-deprecating, flamboyant, declamatory—a pattern of contrasts which enhances the encyclopedic structure and points forward to the marvelous miscellany of *Moby-Dick.*

II

Redburn is a stock figure, the greenhorn country boy who, though perhaps wise to the ways of the woods, is ill-equipped to encounter the wilderness of the cosmopolitan world. But before his tale is told, he has run the initiatory gauntlet of that world and, although not completely rid of his youthful idealism, is at least on the way toward maturity. The framework for this progression consists of six movements: departure from home; arrival in New York; life aboard ship; experiences in England; life aboard ship (2); and arrival in New York. Midway through the fourth movement Redburn meets Harry Bolton, who introduces him to sinful London. There, Harry is the knowing one, Redburn still the innocent. But the episode is concluded when Harry ships aboard Redburn's vessel, for there the American is at home, the Englishman a stranger. It is by this device that Melville gives the book a thematic consistency and demonstrates, as well, the relativity of "innocence."

Another important device is Redburn's grey shooting jacket: at once a memento of past wealth and present poverty, it is also an index of the hero's progress, like the great burden carried by Bunyan's Christian. It is part and parcel of the machinery of traditional allegory—evidence of the loss permitting gain. It is a hunting jacket because, like the gun that Redburn carries with him when he leaves home, it is a sign that the hero is a representative of Young America, an up-country yokel equipped for the "wilds of this wild countree" but hardly prepared to meet the wiles of this wily world. The gun and the jacket, familiar objects in the country, become eccentric properties in the city and on the sea. Once symbols of pride, they become instruments of humiliation.

Having been shamefully divested of his gun, Redburn next comes in for a ribbing on account of his unsuitable jacket, and, in the midst of his early ordeals aboard the *Highlander*, is "baptized over again" as "Buttons," because of the fancy, fox-faced ornaments on his coat. Armor ashore, the shooting jacket becomes a shirt of Nessus afloat: "It pinch[ed] me under the arms, and it vexed, irritated, and tormented me every way" (p. 74). When he first comes aboard, it is the fancy unsuitableness of the coat which draws ridicule to Redburn, but as time passes, the garment undergoes a sea change: "Every day it grew smaller and smaller, particularly after a rain, until at last I thought it would completely exhale, and leave nothing but the bare seams, by way of a skeleton, on my back" (p. 74).

By the time Redburn reaches Liverpool, the fine jacket of time past is little better than rags. A token of discarded boyhood, it is also a reminder of his present condition and becomes a target for scorn all over again. Traipsing through the inhospitable English countryside, Redburn is full of "sad thoughts concerning the cold charities of the world, and the infamous reception given to hapless young travelers in broken-down shooting-jackets" (p. 213). The paradox is heightened by Redburn's comical attempts to rise above his appearance, to retrieve the respect due his gentle birth. Among the "red cheeks and roses" of an English cottage he strives "to talk in Addisonian English, and ere long could see very plainly that my polished phrases were making a surprising impression, though that miserable shooting-jacket of mine was a perpetual drawback to my claims to gentility" (pp. 213–14). Once a symbol of past wealth—pretentious and useless—the jacket becomes a shabby emblem of Redburn's poverty and a demonstration of the standards by which the world judges worth.

Above all else, however, the tattered jacket is the enveloping womb of transformation, the wrapper from which Redburn is delivered into manhood. An emblem of mutability, like the old guidebook that served the boy's dead father, it is useless in the ever-renewing world of *now:* "Yes, the thing that had guided the father could not guide the son. And I sat down on a shop step, and gave loose to meditation" (p. 157). As a token of the innocent past brought into the wiser present, the jacket is a symbol of "self," an emblem of psychical metamorphosis, a blazon which accompanies the rite of passage, the shock of entrance into an indifferent world outside the home circle. It is this symbolic level which gives meaning to "the great castle or fort, all in ruins, and with the trees growing round it" which Redburn's ship passes as it sails out of the "Narrows" into the open sea, one of those circular configurations containing an impossible vision of happiness which continually plague Melville's questers.

The sight of the castle and the memory of the hidden garden within it cause the boy to be overwhelmed with homesickness, for the ruins are a contagious reminder of the past: "It was a beautiful place, as I remembered it, and very wonderful and romantic, too, as it appeared to me, when I went there with my uncle" (p. 35). Like the whale circle, the garden concealed within the old fort is a center of tranquility, a symbol of all that Redburn must leave behind. It is a type of heart garden, entered through a tunnel whose archway is sheltered by a grove of trees, a devious entrance reminiscent of the tunnel leading into the valley of Willamilla. It is "dark as night; and going in, you groped about in long vaults, twisting and turning on every side, till at last you caught a peep of green grass and sunlight, and all at once came out in an open space in the middle of the castle" (p. 35). The experience resembles that of Lombardo, for at the heart of the castle, as in the heart of the poet, all is idyllic, "a beautiful, quiet, charming spot. . . . It was noon-day when I was there, in the month of June, and there was little wind to stir the trees, and everything looked as if it was waiting for something, and the sky overhead was blue as my mother's eye, and I was so glad and happy then" (pp. 35–36).

But the garden in the fort is neither the omphalic valley of Willamilla nor the coefficient of creation. It is a figuration of the cradling womb, the womb not of actual birth (though suggesting that), but of the past, of childhood, a kind of Eden or Arcadia presided over by a loving, motherly eye. It is the womb of comfort from which Redburn is being hurried (down the "Narrows") by the forces of necessity, a token of the memories which will keep him company to the grave, and it provides paradoxical contrast to Redburn's present pain. As Redburn is swept through the Narrows to still another world, he would like to return to the past, to the simple world of memory, but the ship that bears him moves steadily out to sea, like Breughel's little boat that, ignorant of Icarus' fall, sails "out into the broad highway, where not a soul is to be seen." This is the passage out, and "not a voyage complete"; there is no turning back until the journey is over, marking the completion of a new cycle of experience. Pushed out of the Narrows towards the unknown, carried by necessity along the line decreed by Fate, Redburn passes the circular garden to which he can never return, the contentment he must abjure forever.

As the garden in the fort symbolizes the innocent bliss of time past, so a second garden which Redburn encounters symbolizes the viciousness of time present, the two providing the balance of contrast that is characteristic of Melville's ironic diagram, a balance also tokened by the two characters associated with the different gardens—Redburn and Harry Bolton. With Harry as his guide, Redburn is drawn swiftly into the second garden, "whirled along through boundless landscapes of villages, and meadows, and parks: and over arching viaducts, and through wonderful tunnels; till, half delirious with excitement, I found myself dropped down in the evening among gaslights, under a great roof in Euston Square" (p. 226). The wonder of the trip soon changes to apprehension, for the "snow-white" floor of the luxurious gambling house to which he is taken "echoed to the tread, as if all the Paris catacombs were underneath. I started with misgivings at that hollow, boding sound, which seemed sighing with a subterraneous despair, through all the magnificent spectacle around me; mocking it, where most it glared" (p. 228).

Unlike the simple Arcadia inside the old castle, the hidden garden of the gambling house is an artificial monstrosity of gilt and marble, comparable to the ornate room in which the mute maiden of the "Fragment" is discovered. Like that chamber, it is an Acrasian bower, planted with insinuating diction which suggests deception, mimicry, similitude—"sculptured . . . vine-boughs," "mimic grapes," and "porcelain moons"—hints that all is counterfeit, illusory, false. In the Narrows, Redburn wanted to return to the garden past which he was moving, but here he feels nothing but a loathing desire to escape. As the first garden signaled the first step of Redburn's initiation, here, amid oriental trumpery, voluptuousness, and corruption, he reaches the nadir of his experience, a polar opposite to the idyllic garden of youth.

Curiously enough, it is this garden which Harry Bolton is forced to leave, and as the garden in the fort suggests Redburn's essential innocence, so the oriental garden stands for the viciousness of Harry's background. Redburn, fortified by his country upbringing, is able to adapt to the rigors of shipboard life, while Harry, with his corrupt background, can only endure them until he is killed by them. This would seem to imply an absolute interpretation, a variation on the theme established on the American stage as early as Royall Tyler's *The Contrast*. Few of Melville's readers would have been shocked by Redburn's common-sense separation from his decadent European companion at the end of the voyage: " 'Now, my dear friend,' said I, 'Take my advice, and while I am gone, keep up a stout heart; never despair, and all will be well' " (p. 310). Which farewell, like the lawyer's similar admonitions to Bartleby, serves best to substantiate Redburn's earlier aphorism, "it may be, that we should distrust that man's sincerity who stoops to condole with us" (p. 279). The irony implied in Redburn's farewell appears to qualify the apparent improvement in his character. Although he has grown more mature, although he has adjusted to life in the forecastle and has seen the miseries suffered by his fellow men, still he remains essentially a prig at heart. It is by this means that the apparent line of Redburn's development is brought full spiral.

III

Superficially, *White-Jacket* seems to resemble closely its predecessor. Like Redburn, the narrator is a novice, "a sailor altogether unused to the tumult of a man-of-war, for the first time stepping on board," and like him also, "he must begin anew. He knows nothing" (p. 12). Like Redburn's shooting jacket, the canvas grego which he makes for himself is the token of his greenness, serving as well to isolate him from most of the other sailors. This situation, as in *Redburn*, permits some comic episodes, and, when White-Jacket is threatened with a flogging for not knowing his battle station, results in a nearly tragic event. But the emphasis in *White-Jacket* is the reverse of that in *Redburn*: there, all episodes relate to the narrator's development; here, the narrator's development is the excuse for the inclusive examination of all aspects of shipboard life, a microcosmic, cumulative progress which provides the narrative with several levels of intimation. In *Redburn*, similarly, the irony is pointed inward towards the naïvely indignant narrator, but in *White-Jacket* the satire is chiefly at the expense of the man-of-war world.

As the narrative progresses, it becomes clear that the book is not merely an outraged exposé of tyrannical practices in the United States Navy; the attack on the world aboard a man-of-war is also an attack on the wrongs of mankind in general. Like the tour of the Mardian archipelago, the planetary method of the episodic chapters evokes the totality of the world, an evocation reinforced by a series of microcosmic allusions: "A ship is a bit of terra firma cut off from the main; it is a state in itself; and the captain is its king" (p. 23). At times the figures seem almost Homeric in elevation, suggesting the epical language of *Moby-Dick*: "As Richard Nevil entrenched himself in his moated old man-of-war castle of Warwick, which, underground, was traversed with vaults, hewn out of the solid rock, and intricate as the wards of the old keys of Calais, surrendered to Edward III; even so do these King-Commodores house themselves in their water-rimmed, cannon-sentried frigates, oaken dug, deck under deck, as cell under cell" (p. 284). But here, as there, the analogies have a mocking quality, for they serve to underline the paradox of an autocratic reign aboard a ship owned by the people of the United States.

Continuing the microcosmic metaphor, but in contrast to the regal allusions, is a series of domestic analogies. The conversion of the ship for battle is compared to the opening of a mansion's folding doors for "a grand entertainment" (p. 68), and officers preparing for battle by dressing in silk stockings are compared to dandies preparing for a ball. Sailors cleaning the decks of snow are like "rival shop-boys . . . at work cleaning the sidewalk" on Broadway (p. 117), and as they lean on the rail to view the beautiful bay of Rio, they are compared to spectators "lounging round a circular cosmorama, and ever and anon lazily peeping through the glasses here and there" (p. 172). The jocular tone of the narrator scarcely conceals the irony of his analogies, and certain of them carry a serious burden of implication. Thus the ship after battle looks like "West Broadway in New York, after being broken into and burned out by the Negro Mob" (p. 69), and the glow from a phosphorescent sea illuminates the sailors' faces "as a night fire in a populous city lights up the panic-stricken crowd"

(p. 106). When the hated order to shave off their beards is given to the sailors, the tumult is compared to "a populous street of brokers, when some terrible commercial tidings have newly arrived" (p. 357). Each analogy, by calling attention to some social canker, further points up the paradox of American citizens serving aboard "a sort of State Prison" (p. 175), free men forced into unbearable restraint by archaic laws.

These Homeric and domestic similes permit White-Jacket's conclusion that "a man-of-war is but this old-fashioned world of ours afloat, full of all manner of characters—full of strange contradictions; and though boasting some fine fellows here and there, yet, upon the whole, charged to the combings of her hatchways with the spirit of Belial and all unrighteousness" (p. 390). The key words here are "old-fashioned," "strange contradictions," and "unrighteousness," for despite the universal metaphor which it permits, the military microcosm is a specific demonstration that an autocratic system intensifies man's potential for evil. Thus, in attacking the custom of giving boyish midshipmen authority over full-grown enlisted men, White-Jacket declares, "Since what human nature is, and what it must forever continue to be, is well enough understood for most practical purposes, it needs no special example to prove that, where the merest boys, indiscriminately snatched from the human family, are given such authority over mature men, the results must be proportionable in monstrousness to the custom that authorizes this worse than cruel absurdity" (p. 218). In other words, the unnatural order of the ("old-fashioned") military organization allows for, rather than restrains, man's innate capacity for vice (a "strange contradiction"). Military ("unrighteous") order with its devices for restraint and discipline is actually an instrument of misrule, permitting the upset of natural patterns of life.

The most egregious examples of misrule aboard the Neversink are the master-at-arms, Bland, and the ship's surgeon, Cadwallader Cuticle. The one engages in illegal activities while charged with enforcing the Articles of War; the other uses his position as healer

to carry out sadistic, useless operations. Bland, superficially regarded, is an attractive person, a Chesterfieldian sailor who bows
and smiles "to right and left, as if springy, bouyant, and elastic,
with an angelic conscience, and sure of kind friends wherever he
went, both in this life and the life to come" (p. 187). But he also
has a glittering eye, a treacherously arched mouth, and "wickedly
delicate" features, suggesting that his gentlemanliness is that of
the "Devil himself . . . free, fine, and frank" (p. 188). This
coupling of gentlemanly characteristics and a villainous nature is
not limited to the man-of-war world ("Ashore, such a man might
have been an irreproachable mercantile swindler, circulating in
polite society"), and yet Bland's masquerade "furnishes the most
curious evidence of the almost incredible corruption pervading
nearly all ranks in some men-of-war." For this "ineffable villain" is
a favorite of the captain's, having presented him with a "rare snuffbox" and "a splendid gold-mounted cane" several months before
his arrest for smuggling brandy aboard the *Neversink*. While the
other guilty sailors were flogged and confined in chains, the master-
at-arms was "merely cashiered and imprisoned for a time, with
bracelets at his wrists," and was eventually restored to his original,
law-enforcing office, letting "him entirely loose to prey upon
honest seamen, fore and aft all three decks," much as the Devil is
permitted by God to walk up and down in the world, and to and
fro in it.

If the master-at-arms is the Devil, then the surgeon is his
dancing partner, Death. A "singularly attenuated" skeleton of a
man, with much of his bodily substance wasted away or entirely
missing, he yet retains an incongruous spark of intelligence, his
single eye burning "with basilisk brilliance." Cuticle is a walking
intellect, a man of science whose cruel, killing eye denies his
assumed title of healer, a chilling personification of annihilatory
power. The "withered, shrunken, one-eyed, toothless, hairless
Cuticle" is "a *memento mori* to behold!" (p. 259). Like Ahab, he
is "a trunk half-dead," a burnt-out case of misbegotten zeal, who

uses his superior rank to force his opinion and slay yet another
victim under the guise of curing him.

There would seem to be an implicit comparison between the
Articles of War and the Constitution of the United States, with
its careful balance of powers designed to protect men from themselves. For surely the greatest absurdity of the military system is
that it is enforced on a ship owned by the people of the United
States: "While the Neversink was in the Pacific, an American
sailor, who had deposited a vote for General Harrison for President of the United States, was flogged through the fleet" (p.
372). This playing off of democratic ideals (the rights of the
people) against military realities (the abuses inflicted upon the
"people") is a political paradox. In turn it is supported by a religious paradox, in which the tyrannical Articles of War are
compared to the gentle admonitions of the Sermon on the Mount.
Of the two, concludes White-Jacket wryly, it is the Articles which
are "an index to the true condition of the present civilization of
the world" (p. 293), for a world which can produce the conditions
on a man-of-war is not yet ready for the message of the man of
peace.

The political paradox is pointed up by the contrasting characters
of Jack Chase (a natural leader) and Captain Claret (an incompe-
tent leader appointed through political favoritism). That Jack
Chase has the ability to become an officer is demonstrated by the
incident in which he deserts his ship temporarily to become a
lieutenant in the Peruvian Navy. The incompetence of Captain
Claret is similarly displayed when, in rounding Cape Horn, he
nearly sinks his ship by a hasty and drink-befuddled order. Again,
the underlying irony is twofold. There is the paradox of a system
which allows incompetence in office, a system which also forbids
an enlisted man, however well qualified, to cross the barrier of
rank: "Any American landsman may hope to become President of
the Union—commodore of our squadron of states," but "it is a
great reproach that such a thing as a common seaman rising to the

rank of a commissioned officer in our Navy is nowadays almost unheard-of" (p. 114).

The religious paradox, first suggested by a peep into the ward room, where White-Jacket spies "the chaplain . . . playing chess with the Lieutenant of Marines" (p. 24), is given point by the fact of the chaplain himself, a man of God aboard a ship of war (an irony increased by the clergyman's incompetence as a minister to ignorant sailors). This paradox is summarized in Chapter 76, "The Chains," an emblematic digression in which the peculiar social environment of the man-of-war world occasions a metaphor which in turn allows a short sermon on the unsuitability of Christ's teachings in a world which permits wars to continue, the real point of which is that those teachings have nothing to do with the world of men.

"The Chains" further serves as a summary statement of the conditions of life aboard a warship. The title of the chapter is taken from the name of the "small platform outside of the hull, at the base of the large shrouds leading down from the three mast-heads to the bulwarks," which the sailors find to be the most "agreeable retreat" aboard the *Neversink*. It is here that they "lazily lounge—outside of the ship, though on board" (p. 323). But, as the ominous name of their "retreat" suggests, the sailors' leisure is a limited one, and though they may imagine themselves outside the ship, they are still very much aboard it, chained fast to the Articles of War. A final twist is provided by the number of the "Chains" chapter—76—a number sacred to the principles of individual liberty and the founding principles of national democracy.

IV

It is this tension between the individual's desire for privacy and the tendency of the military system to violate that privacy which eventually brings White-Jacket into confrontation with the system within which he is forced to live, though as an outcast and alien. For the chief emblem of violation is the cat-o'-nine-tails, and much is made of this weapon of tyranny in the central chapters 33 through 36, which offer preparation for the climactic episode in which White-Jacket himself is nearly stripped and flogged. Generally at the periphery of action, observing but seldom participating, White-Jacket is suddenly thrust into the very center of the stage, a shivering victim of the tyranny which he has been describing.

As the "Chains" are an emblem of the paradoxical existence of the crew, the grego which gives White-Jacket his name is a token of his own enigmatic dilemma, at once a sign of personal identity and of his loathed military existence. When he first designs the jacket, it seems a model of utility, comfort, and privacy, but, for the lack of a coat of waterproof black, it soon becomes a sponge to the elements, and, because of the persistence of shipboard pickpockets, its commodious "pantries" become useless for storing valuables. Even more important, because of its "white as a shroud" color, it becomes an object of superstitious aversion for the crew. In short, like Redburn's jacket, the grego becomes the antithesis of what it was meant to be, an acute reminder of its owner's sense of being out of place.

Unlike Redburn's hunting jacket, however, the grego is not a wrapper of transformation. The emphasis in *White-Jacket* is not on the narrator's metamorphosis into an experienced sailor (he is already that), but on his attempts to remain an individual while yet seeking the acceptance of the crew. The difficulty of such a divided quest in the warship world of regulations and uniformity is emphasized by the singular white-jacket: though the jacket certainly accentuates the narrator's individuality, in so doing it also serves to alienate him from most of his shipmates. Lacking the charismatic qualities of a Jack Chase, an ordinary sailor like White-Jacket finds that to be an individual is to be an outcast. Because of the unique jacket, he is "blackballed" from his assigned mess, mistaken for a ghost and almost killed, continually singled out for errands and abuse by the petty officers, and wrongly blamed by a superstitious gunner's mate for the death of a shipmate. His efforts to darken the jacket are ineffectual, and its inutilitarian bulkiness is nearly the death of him. The ordered world of the man-of-war is concentric, and the eccentric individual ships aboard at great hazard. Though the world may be a sum of contradictory parts, it does not do to be a contradiction of the total sum. The safest course (that taken by the reclusive afterguardsman, Nord) is to assume the protective coloration of anonymity, but this White-Jacket cannot do, and for his failure he is punished.

Despite White-Jacket's acceptance by Jack Chase and the aristocrats of the foretop, his coat continues to bring him discomfort and eventually becomes a token of his new and loathed identity, the white stigma of his pariahdom. Though White-Jacket tries to rid himself of it, it remains with him until the end of the voyage, when, having been the cause of his near fatal fall from a yardarm, it is shed for good and all: "Sink! sink! oh shroud! thought I; sink forever! accursed jacket that thou art!" (p. 394). The jacket, at first emblematic of White-Jacket's heart (open, roomy, comfortable), has come to stand for the man-of-war world (closed, restrictive, uncomfortable, dangerous), and by shedding it, he bids that world farewell. In the next chapter, the narrative is hurried to a conclusion, thus coupling the loss of the jacket with the arrival of the *Neversink* in the United States and White-Jacket's departure from the hated microcosm. With the removal of the jacket the narrator is not changed—he is merely returned to freedom. Once before he was threatened with the loss of his jacket—when ordered up for a flogging by Captain Claret. But this stripping is the antithesis of that other (though associated also with death by drowning), and by accomplishing it, White-Jacket leaves all that the captain stood for behind him.

Chapter Five

Moby-Dick:
Line and Circle

Ahab's quest dominates the narrative advance of *Moby-Dick,*
but it is Ishmael who corresponds at the outset to Melville's
earlier questers, Tommo and Taji. It is he who is "tormented
with an everlasting itch for things remote," who hopes to escape
melancholy by quitting the crowds of water-gazers and going to
sea as a sailor. He is an adventurer who loves "to sail forbidden
seas, and land on barbarous coasts" (p. 6), and the threshold to
adventure is New Bedford, prophetically gloomy, with dark,
tomblike streets. Entering what he assumes is an inn, Ishmael
stumbles into the pitchy blackness of a Negro church, like the
"great Black Parliament sitting in Tophet" (p. 8). This somber
omen is darkened further by the implications of the signboard
on the Spouter Inn: "Coffin?—Spouter?—Rather ominous in that
particular connexion, thought I"; and the first thing that catches
Ishmael's eye as he enters the inn is a prophetic picture with "a
long, limber, portentous, black mass of something hovering in the
centre" (p. 10).

But with the characteristic optimism of Melville's questers,
Ishmael shrugs off the Black Parliament and the "black mass"
alike and cheerfully beds down with a South Seas savage who
resembles "the devil himself" (p. 21). He awakes to find Queequeg's arm thrown over him "in the most loving and affectionate

manner," but this "bridegroom clasp" holds him "as though naught but death should part us." Ishmael is reminded by his helpless situation of a childhood experience, in which he awoke to find his hand held by a "nameless, unimaginable, silent form or phantom." Perhaps the consoling spirit of his dead mother, the "supernatural hand" caused nothing but fear in the boy, who lay frozen and unable to move, much as the older Ishmael is trapped by a savage arm "tattooed all over with an interminable Cretan labyrinth of a figure," emblematic of the mazelike world in which they will both go questing for a deadly white Minotaur (pp. 25–26).

The conjunction of hand, arm, and labyrinth is another dark portent, but Ishmael disregards them all, putting his faith in "a good laugh," which is "a mighty good thing, and rather too scarce a good thing" (p. 29). Having attended church with Queequeg, he joins his bosom friend in worshipping a pagan idol, an easy relativism that is typical of Ishmael, for whom "there is no quality in this world that is not what it is merely by contrast" (p. 53), who would rather sleep with a sober cannibal than a drunken Christian, and for whom the will of God is "to do to my fellow man what I would have my fellow man do to me" (p. 52). It is this same relativism that allows Ishmael to recognize "the endlessness, yea, the intolerableness of all earthly effort," while spurning "turnpike earth" for the "magnanimity of the sea" (p. 59).

This seagoing spirit is epitomized by Bulkington, a symbolic figure like Queequeg, who also becomes Ishmael's shipmate. Bulkington's Byronic avoidance of the "lee shore," his seeking of "all the lashed sea's landlessness, for refuge's sake forlornly rushing into peril" is the apotheosis of the questing spirit, exemplified in the succeeding narrative by Captain Ahab. Like Ahab, Bulkington represents "that mortally intolerable truth; that all deep, earnest thinking is but the intrepid effort of the soul to keep the open independence of her sea, while the wildest winds of heaven and earth conspire to cast her on the treacherous, slavish shore" (p. 105). Sharing this spirit, at least for the time being, Ishmael sails with Queequeg from New Bedford to Nantucket, an inner

island" that is the jumping-off place to infinity, whose inhabitants can sleep with gull-like tranquility while afloat on the ocean, as under their "very pillows rush herds of walruses and whales" (p. 63).

But the tranquility of the gull is illusory, Bulkington finally drowns, and Ishmael's choice of the barbarous *Pequod* as a vessel for adventure is shadowed by the forboding thresholds over which he has passed: "It's ominous, thinks I" (p. 63). Ominous too are certain prophetic voices. The lesson of Father Mapple's "two-stranded" sermon is that one should please and obey God while yet preaching "the Truth to the face of Falsehood!" One thinks of Ahab when Father Mapple promises delight to him who "against the proud gods and commodores of this earth, ever stands forth his own inexorable self," but the other strand, that "if we obey God, we must disobey ourselves; and it is in this disobeying ourselves, wherein the hardness of obeying God consists," reveals the ungodliness of Ahab's egoism, the essential blasphemy of his quest (pp. 48, 41). Ahab is a paradox, a "fighting Quaker," a "Quaker with a vengeance," whose reliance on inner convictions has been drastically "modified by individual circumstances" (p. 73). Doomed and damned, Ahab and his quest receive a twisted benediction by the crazed Elijah, whose "ambiguous, half-hinting, half-revealing, shrouded sort of talk" inspires in Ishmael "all kinds of vague wonderments and half-apprehensions," but they are all passed off finally by him as "humbug" (pp. 93–94).

On Christmas Eve, the crew having given "three heavy-hearted cheers," the *Pequod* "blindly plunged like fate into the lone Atlantic," with Ishmael and his barbaric bridegroom on board. From this point on, following the "Lee Shore" and the apotheosis of Bulkington, the quest is taken over by Ahab, Ishmael serving as chronicler, lexicographer, and oarsman. For Ahab is the "Captain," while humbler Ishmael has "gone to sea as a sailor," and his quest is absorbed in Ahab's, whose mad search for the White Whale comes in time to seem his own. And yet, as a common sailor, Ishmael retains something of Sancho Panza's cowardice and common sense, and while "all a-rush to encounter the whale, could see naught in that brute but the deadliest ill" (p. 185). Admiring Ahab, fearing him, Ishmael makes his presence known by means of the cetology chapters. And by hinting at the ultimate futility of the quest, he joins the party of prophetic Fedallah and mad little Pip, who cryptically predict the captain's death.

II

The device of countering Ishmael's adventurous urgings by a series of ominous episodes gives way to a much more complicated arrangement, in which Ahab's absolutistic quest is qualified by the various attitudes towards the White Whale voiced by the *Pequod's* crew (a version of symposium) and the several world views suggested by the various whalers with which Ahab's ship has contact. But the most important planetary device is provided by the cetology chapters. Ahab's quest is associated with the kinetic, linear element of the story—the onrushing narrative. The cetology chapters, with their relatively static, discursive movements, act to block and impede the forward movement of the narrative, much as the ideas which they contain qualify Ahab's absolutism.

At first glance, the encyclopedic cetology chapters seem to promote the macrocosmic significance of Moby Dick. By marshaling historical and mythological materials associated, however remotely, with whales and whaling, they act as epic similes to elevate the subject of whales until the object-Whale of Ahab's quest becomes one with the universe. As Ahab's mad subjectivity creates a symbol of universal malignity, Ishmael's rational relativity creates a universe of being, of *All,* which inflates even further the importance of Moby Dick, the giant among whales. But even as they built up the White Whale's significance, assisting in the metamorphosis of phenomenon to noumenon, the cetology chapters act to negate the validity of Ahab's hunt. Much of what Ishmael says about whales is factitious, from his insistence that the whale is a fish to his insistence that Perseus was the first whale-

man. This direction is mock heroic, mock epical, and qualifies the
validity of Ahab's heroic character and the epical nature of his
quest. Moreover, by collective implication these chapters suggest
that the Whale can never be "known" (i.e., caught), that as a
symbol of the universe he shares the puzzlelike nature of the
universe and is shadowy, elusive, paradoxical, inscrutable. Ahab,
who tries to impose an absolute interpretation on Moby Dick, fails
to read the puzzle rightly, and yet Moby Dick's savage retaliation
suggests that the captain is not entirely wrong, either. Like the
Whale, the book is a cipher also, the result of paired possibilities
and unreconcilable opposites.

Though Ishmael and Ahab never meet face to face, they are
engaged in a long debate, and, as in a debate, their arguments
enhance yet refute one another. Ahab reduces Moby Dick to an
analogy of his mad idea of nature, making inscrutable blankness a
mask of universal malice. Ishmael, though suspecting a fearful
contingency, suspects nature to be at base a hollow sham, hiding
absolutely nothing. He discourses not only on the whiteness that is
to him symbolic of the "atheistical" void behind appearances, but
on man's many futile attempts to arrive at some common agreement as to the nature of appearances, attempts which, when
opposed one to one, add up (like the implications of whiteness) to
absolute zero. Whereas Ahab hopes to end his pursuit with the
capture of Moby Dick, Ishmael fears that the chase has but three
possibilities, none fruitful: it will end where it began; it will lose
itself in the world-maze; it will end in disaster.

The opposition of Ahab and Ishmael is one of character type
(misanthrope and philanthrope), ontology (absolutist and relativist), and psychology (head and heart). Ahab's reasoning is
deductive; Ishmael's is inductive. Ahab's personality is fixed, virtually unwavering, while Ishmael is moody, contradictory. The
scheme is not perfect (thank goodness!), for Ishmael is fascinated
by the "idea" of the Whale and is swayed by Ahab's rhetoric into
joining the fiery hunt. Ahab, on the other hand, has his "humani-
ties" and his moments of self-doubt. But these exceptions serve

only to achieve a larger end, to dovetail points of view, welding the opposition of attitudes into an impervious unity, an organic puzzle which contains the complexity of the world.

Whereas Ahab considers himself to be the captain of his own soul, only at the last moment acknowledging the possibility that "we are turned round and round in this world, like yonder windlass, and Fate is the handspike" (p. 536), Ishmael from the very beginning conceives himself in the charge of "the invisible police officer of the Fates, who has the constant surveillance of me, and secretly dogs me, and influences me in some unaccountable way" (p. 5). Though an adventurer, he is an advocate of home and hearth as well. Realizing that there are spheres of fright as well as spheres of love, that "there is a wisdom that is woe; but there is a woe that is madness," that "when on one side you hoist in Locke's head, you go over that way; but now, on the other side, hoist in Kant's and you come back again," Ishmael is an equilibrist: "Doubts of all things earthly, and intuitions of some things heavenly; this combination makes neither believer nor infidel, but makes a man who regards them both with equal eye" (pp. 193, 423, 326, 372).

This opposition of character traits is part of the ironic diagram, an association that extends even to metaphor. Relativistic Ishmael with his relativistic cetology chapters is an exponent of circular views. He hopes "to include the whole circle of the sciences, and all the generations of whales, and men, and mastodons, past, present, and to come, with all the revolving panoramas of empire on earth, and throughout the whole universe, not excluding its suburbs" within his book (p. 452). Not only may the cetology chapters be seen as circular in implication, but Ishmael's journey, unlike Ahab's, is a round trip. He is often associated with circular objects, like the tubs of sperm, or holistic events, like the invasion of the whale circle. At the outset, he identifies himself with the "insular city of the Manhattoes, belted round by wharves as Indian isles by coral reefs—commerce surround[ing] it with her surf," a centrifuge on whose outer rim "all around" stand thousands of sea dreamers, and which is an emblem of the "round world itself." And at the end of the book, Ishmael is found bobbing on the rim of the creamy vortex left by the sinking *Pequod.*

Absolutistic Ahab, contrarily, is associated with lines. According to the prophetic old carpenter, Ahab is "always under the Line— fiery hot, I tell ye!" (p. 520), an analogy echoed in the mad captain's plan to meet with Moby Dick during the "Season-on-the-Line." His figure, too, is linear, a quixotic leanness that suggests the intensity of his enthusiast conviction. He is wasted and gaunt, "like a man cut away from the stake," and his "whole high, broad form, seem[s] made of solid bronze" (p. 120). The mark of his casting is a "slender, rod-like scar" which is rumored to run the length of his body and which terminates in the ivory stick-leg fixed in an auger hole bored into Ahab's quarter-deck. Stationed there, his body fastened to the body of his ship, Ahab presents a figurehead portrait of single-mindedness, imagery enhanced by alliteration: "His bone leg steadied in that hole; one arm elevated, and holding by a shroud; Captain Ahab stood erect, looking straight out beyond the ship's ever-pitching prow. There was an infinity of firmest fortitude, a determinate, unsurrenderable wilfulness, in the fixed and fearless, forward dedication of that glance" (pp. 122–23).

Clinging to a prophetic "shroud" (portent of the hempen line that is to strangle him), and bracing himself against the eternal rolling of the sea by means of an "auger" hole and a "bone" leg, Ahab imagines himself master of his fate. He compares himself to an express train, that technical marvel, and, with his faith in himself and his ship, is an insane epitome of Western man, whose faith is in linear progress, whose wisdom is based upon analogies. For Ahab, the world is an allegory in which Moby Dick is a personification of malignity, a diagon needing a knight to slaughter it. But for Ishmael, whose consciousness has an Eastern awareness of relativity, of the endlessly revolving cycles of time, the Whale (whose very name means "roundness or rolling") is a totality of meaningless impressions, a something that is nothing, a symbol of the void at the center of material reality. And for Ishmael the line on which Ahab hopes to meet the Whale is really a circle, for any line on "this round globe" leads us "only through numberless perils to the very point whence we started, where those that we left behind secure, were all the time before us" (p. 236).

III

Circle and line merge in the symbolism of the doubloon which Ahab nails to the mast as a prize for the man who first sights Moby Dick. All the major characters (save Ishmael) confront the coin, and all interpret it in the light of their particular biases, for like the Whale, the doubloon is an index of truth's relativity. It is the "white whale's talisman" and takes its significance from his essential mystery. Both by its "thingness" and by its predominant symbol—"the keystone sun entering the equinoctial point at Libra"—the coin is an emblem of transcendent, planetary power, a sun token, made from gold mined and minted under the equator (p. 428). But this token of balance has been nailed to the mast by a monomaniac who regards the equator as a "line," and who confronts the coin's golden roundness with a dark intensity of purpose: "When he halted before the binnacle, with his glance fastened on the pointed needle in the compass, that glance shot like a javelin with the pointed intensity of his purpose; and when resuming his walk he again paused before the mainmast, then, as the same riveted glance fastened upon the riveted gold coin there, he still wore the same aspect of nailed firmness, only dashed with a certain wild longing, if not hopefulness" (p. 427). As Ahab ignores the roundness of binnacle and compass rose for the pointed needle, so he ignores the implications of the round coin. As he has nailed it, so would he like to nail Moby Dick, to pierce him with the harpoon that is the chief instrument of his "pointed intensity."

So monomaniacal is Ahab that to him even the symbols on the

coin correspond to aspects of his ego. In his view, it is an absolute, not a relativistic, token—as Moby Dick seems to him a symbol of universal malevolence, so the various signs on the coin stand for various aspects of his own personality. But the coin (like the Whale) transcends Ahab's interpretation of it. The generic symbols on its face draw together the various ontological strands of the book into one mysterious Gordian knot: the "Andes" summit, crowned by a flame, suggests the hell-fire of the tryworks episode, the madness of introversion, while the mountain bearing a tower hints at the airy pantheism of the masthead incident. And the crowing cock on the third mountain is a blazon of egotism, a "cock-of-the-walk." Each of the three suggests some extreme viewpoint, but all three "heaven-abiding" peaks are joined at a common base in the "dark valley" of doubt, and the dominant sun is frozen in the balance sign of Libra. Minted under the equator, the doubloon gathers and equates the disparate opinions of the crew towards the Whale and contains (joins) antipodes of existential attitude. A unity forged of disunities, the coin is a puzzle whose meaning can only be read by little Pip, for whom the heroic captain is an object of jeering laughter.

Ahab may have nailed the coin to the mast, but Pip prophesies that it is the captain who will be nailed by Moby Dick. Pip has experienced the huge extremity of the ocean, a golden circle of infinity "flatly stretching away, all round . . . like gold beater's skin hammered out to the extremest" (p. 412). Pip, "from the centre of the sea," has turned his head to the sun, "another lonely castaway, though the loftiest and brightest," having returned from darkest depths; and floating in "the middle of such a heartless immensity," centered within a golden circle, he has gained the ultimate wisdom granted here on earth: "Man's insanity is heaven's sense; and wandering from all mortal reason, man comes at last to that celestial thought, which, to reason, is absurd and frantic; and weal or woe, feels then uncompromised, indifferent as his God" (p. 413). To the mad, withdrawn, and indifferent Pip, the mad reasonableness of Ahab's analogies seems like the plan of a fool who "wol sleen this false traytour Deeth. He shal be slayn, he that so manye sleeth!"

Mad Ahab is the first to interpret the coin's symbols, and the demented Negro is the last. According to Pip, the doubloon is "the ship's navel . . . and they are all on fire to unscrew it. But, unscrew your navel, and what's the consequence? Then again, if it stays there, that is ugly, too, for when aught's nailed to the mast it's a sign that things grow desperate" (p. 432). The coin is a navel, "contemplated" by each member of the crew in turn—fixed to the center of the ship, it is dominated by "Libra," the navel sign of the zodiacal Great Man. The talisman of the Whale, token of Ahab's quest, the coin is fundamental to the structure of the book and a sign of the universal ambiguity which the book is designed to accommodate. If it should, like the navel of the fabled Hindu which Pip seems to have in mind, be unscrewed, the results would be disastrous.

No one is more on fire to unscrew the golden navel than old Ahab, who wants both Whale and talisman. And in attacking the Whale, in arousing that mystery to show its dark, malevolent side, he attempts to violate the circle of existence, to penetrate the Omphalos, the navel of God. In the end, he does succeed in penetrating the divine helix, but by the only means available to mortal man. Caught in the spiraling threads of a maelstrom, Ahab, his ship, and his crew are drawn down into the depths to death, providing a final configuration of the paradoxical force with which Ishmael has been dealing throughout—the circle which is the antithesis of the line, and its synthesis as well, here on this round globe.

The circular view is transcendental and holds that "Nature is intricate, overlapped, interweaved, and endless." It is tokened by the doubloon, but it is also figured in the sword mat woven by Ishmael and Queequeg. The warp of the loom is necessity, the shuttle is free will, but the pattern of the mat's weave is determined by the blows of "Queequeg's impulsive, indifferent sword" (p. 213), the careless weapon of chance: "Aye, chance, free-will, and necessity—in no wise incompatible—all interweavingly work-ing together," but the greatest of these seems to be chance, for "though thus prescribed to by both, chance by turns rules either, and has the last featuring blow at events." It is chance which determines the pattern of fate, and it is by chance that Ishmael survives the sinking of the *Pequod,* as it is a chance loop of the whale line that snatches Ahab into eternity.

But Ahab's solipsistic view precludes chance. He has chained it to the instruments of his will, the compass needle and his harpoon. His quixotic illusions have become his only reality, for he has yielded up "all his thoughts and fancies to his one supreme pur-pose; [which] purpose, by its own sheer inveteracy of will, forced itself against gods and devils into a kind of self-assumed, inde-pendant being of its own" (p. 200). As Ishmael's stoicism has its diagram in the sword mat, so Ahab's willfulness is mapped by the "pointed intensity of his charts," the sane means by which his mad object is to be accomplished.

Emblematically, the "lines and shadings" on the chart are matched by the "shifting gleams and shadows of lines" thrown on Ahab's wrinkled brow by the heavy lamp "suspended in chains" overhead, "till it almost seemed that while he himself was marking out lines and courses on the wrinkled charts, some invisible pencil was also tracing lines and courses upon the deeply marked chart of his forehead" (p. 195). And Ahab's pale brow, in turn, is reflected in the hieroglyphic markings on the snow-white forehead of the White Whale, suggesting (as with his bone leg) a link of shared identity between fierce Ahab and his ferocious adversary. The lines also indicate a plan of calculated analogies of which the willful Ahab is only a subsidiary part, and of which, because of his single-minded purpose, he is not aware.

The lines on the chart differ from those of the mat in that they disregard the element of chance, and it is here that Ahab makes his fatal mistake. He has put his faith in rational means, in the statistics and records from which his ingenious chart has been constructed, but he has ignored the vagaries of chance. Part of a totality, Ahab cannot transcend the pattern; nor, like Jonah, can he escape it. As Fedallah darkly foresees, Ahab will be strangled by a cord woven in part by himself and compounded of the same strands that go to make up the sword mat—free will, necessity, and chance. The ironic pattern is completed when Ahab, having braved all dangers, conquered all souls, disregarded all portents, encounters his adversary only to be dragged down by his true antagonist, a "chance" loop in the instrument of his revenge—not the dedicated harpoon, but the humble, hempen rope attached to it, the last unraveling of Ahab's linear voyage. That deadly, prophetic hemp, formed of the same stuff as the shroud to which the captain has clung for so long, pulls him down beneath the "great shroud of the sea," which rolls on unheeding, "as it rolled five thousand years ago."

IV

The indifferent, hermaphroditic ocean which swallows Ahab, along with his charts, compass, harpoon, and ship, is a blend of contrasts, shades and gleamings which absorb man's purposeful thread with its great, conjugal harmonies, its symphony of contrasting yet complementary elements:

It was a clear steel-blue day. The firmaments of air and sea were hardly separable in that all-pervading azure; only, the pensive air was transparently pure and soft, with a woman's look, and the robust and man-like sea heaved with long, strong, lingering swells, as Samson's chest in his sleep.

Hither, and thither, on high, glided the snow-white wings of small, unspeckled birds; these were the gentle thoughts of the feminine air; but to and fro in the deeps, far down in the bottomless blue, rushed mighty leviathans, sword-fish, and sharks; and these were the strong, troubled, murderous thinkings of the masculine sea.

But though thus contrasting within, the contrast was only in shades and shadows without; those two seemed one; it was only the sex, as it were, that distinguished them.

Aloft, like a royal czar and king, the sun seemed giving this gentle air to this bold and rolling sea; even as bride to groom. And at the girdling line of the horizon, a soft and tremulous motion—most seen here at the equator—denoted the fond, throbbing trust, the loving alarms, with which the poor bride gave her bosom away (pp. 532–33).

The suggestion here is of a transcendental, Emersonian "All," the benevolent wedding of elements ("at the equator") which Taji extolled in the opening chapters of *Mardi*—a harmonious, affirmative wholeness providing contrast to Ahab's absolutism. But here, as in Melville's other circles, the wholeness is qualified by imagery: as the sharks and other sea monsters qualify, by balancing, the serenity of the sky-borne birds, so the air itself—"steel-blue"—carries a suggestion of threat, particularly when coupled with the image of the sleeping Samson—Delilah, too, was a woman, with "a woman's look." And the loving bride, in giving herself, does so with "alarm," spheres of fright mingling with spheres of love.

Ahab, when confronted with these symphonic, nuptial harmonies, seems a burnt-out case of spent passions, "his eyes glowing like coals, that still glow in the ashes of ruin," perfect contrast to the scene before him. Yet, while the "sweet childhood of air and sky" remains oblivious to "old Ahab's close-coiled woe," the captain for his part responds to the maternal touch of "that glad, happy air, that winsome sky," by dropping a tear into the ocean. Still, the tear is one of self-pity and nostalgia ("On such a day—very much such a sweetness as this—I struck my first whale—a boy harpooneer of eighteen!"), not true realization, and Ahab soon returns to leviathan thoughts and shark sentiments. Crossing to the other side of his ship, he abandons Starbuck for the reflected eyes of Fedallah.

Thus, while constantly reminding us of the eternal flux, of the absence of absolutes, Melville nevertheless returns to the relatively fixed structure of contrasts, line and circle, which lies at the heart of his narrative. The circle may be broken, but to a circle it returns, and the line soon becomes taut again. For Ahab throughout has eyes only for darks and depths, for leviathans and sharkish thoughts—like Narcissus, he mistakes his own dark reflection for truth, "and this is the key to it all." Having converted himself, like his razors, into an instrument of his ruling passion, the captain has become his own fate indeed, but in a sense not realized by himself. The world is a fluid loom through which he drives the shuttle of his quest, but the willful pattern of his plan is ultimately absorbed by the whole, the Whale, the fabric of being constructed from the matched contraries of existence.

Chapter Six

Pierre:
The Structure of Ambiguity

Melville customarily regarded the creative process as organic, and the sequence of his works is consistent with this Coleridgean view. Thus *Mardi* is a romantic elaboration on the exotic materials of *Typee,* and *Moby-Dick* combines elements of both *Mardi* and *White-Jacket* while transcending the derivative parts to become a new creation. And *Pierre,* in its turn, continues to demonstrate Melville's creative dialectic, amplifying still further the possibilities of the ironic diagram.

The quest, as in *Mardi,* is motivated by a mysterious beauty whose power to allure draws an infatuated youth to his destruction, but instead of giving himself up to allegory, Melville stages the quest, as in *Redburn,* as a *Bildungsroman,* a progress from innocence into wisdom, from the idyllic life of the country to the purgatorial existence of the city. Though, like Taji, Pierre undergoes a paradoxical conversion from idealist to nihilist, it is only after a prolonged period of suffering and doubt. Like Ahab, the Pierre of the catastrophe is a "dark," Byronic hero, but unlike Ahab, he is permitted little freedom of movement. Surrounded by antitheses, he is tormented by self-doubt and misgivings about his idealistic quest, until at last, maddened by the implications of ambiguity, he commits the full power of his will to self-destruction, an act paralleling Ahab's final assault upon the Whale. Whereas Ahab has a scapegoat upon which he may project his inner torment, Pierre has only himself to blame, and, forced to descend into his soul, he drowns in the vacuum there.

Although Melville continued to use the romantic quest as a structural device, his characterization of Pierre as a "hamstrung moose" suggests a changing attitude towards the quester. Though Taji and Ahab are doomed to failure from the outset of their voyages, they are permitted a freedom of action and a heroic posture entirely denied Pierre. As in *White-Jacket,* there is little physical movement, and where the hero of the earlier novel is trapped by the confines of a compartmentalized, bureaucratic, and militaristic society, Pierre is caught up in a Laocoön-like tangle of doubts and irresolution. The result is a near stasis, with the consequent diminishing of the linear aspect of the diagram. Pierre seldom goes straight forward, but rather seems to dash himself off the sides of the ambiguities with which he is surrounded.

Related to this shift in attitude is Melville's use of the third-person narrator, here for the first time used throughout. By abstracting the transcendent point of view with which *Moby-Dick* concludes, by elevating the narrator above the adventures of his hero, Melville seems to be disassociating himself from the quest, to be assuming the disinterested pose of complete irony. In each previous effort the viewpoint was in some way associated with the quester, and though—as in *Mardi* and *Moby-Dick*—that association could become tenuous during the course of the narrative, it does suggest an empathic relationship between author and narrator, that the quester is, however much qualified by mockery and counterpoint, the agent of the author's search for truth. By abandoning this stand for a self-conscious narrator—a showman who ubiquitously guides, urges, elucidates, and comments upon the folly of his hero—Melville seems to be identifying himself with the planetary rather than the linear aspect of his diagram. We may feel that the narrator was ironically conceived, that the fortunes of Pierre were too close to Melville's heart to be entirely disavowed, but the terms of the structure undeniably reinforce the possibility of authorial alienation.

Furthermore, save for a definitely ironic use of the first person in a number of short stories (notably the lawyer in "Bartleby"), Melville maintained the third-person viewpoint throughout his subsequent work. As he entered that phase of his career which ends with *The Confidence-Man,* the gap of empathy between narrator and quester continued to widen, each change in attitude moving Melville farther from subjective participation toward disinterested observation. This movement is accompanied by a diminishing of the quester's stature (Ahab to Pierre to Amasa Delano), further evidence that Melville was revising his attitude towards "seekers," was perhaps coming to some reluctant compromise with existence. The nihilism with which he had toyed for so long spreads like an ague through the fibers of his art during the period following *Pierre,* and, with the writing of *The Confidence-Man,* all activity ceases, with character and style solidifying into a perfect cipher of ambiguity.

II

It might be said that the linear aspect of Melville's diagram is associated with the tragic element of his early novels, identified as it is with the noble yet fated quester, while the circle is associated with satire, with the Rabelaisian islands of Mardi or the mocking cetology chapters. This dichotomy is continued in *Pierre,* and although the familiar device of the voyage and a microcosmic Micronesia is missing, it is not difficult to outline its equivalent. On the tragic level, by surrounding his hero with what appear to be the materials of ethical choice, but which are really unfathomable ambiguities, Melville suggests the cosmic hoax of appearances which underlies all tragedy. And by commingling satiric elements with the profounder ambiguities, by ridiculing the specific follies of his hero, of his hero's old world, and of the new world that he enters, Melville unites the two levels of irony. Pierre's final fall is staged amidst a rogues' gallery of tricksters, charlatans, and swindlers.

The result is a tragic version of *Redburn,* for Pierre—like Harry Bolton—cannot come to terms with existence and goes under, while his Redburn-like friend, Charlie Millthorpe, is made of more buoyant stuff ("the glory of the bladder") and survives. Like Ishmael, Charlie floats, and like him also he knows that "The whole world's a trick. Know the trick of it, all's right; don't know, all's wrong. Ha! ha!" (p. 376). As in *Redburn,* also, the action is enhanced by a compensating mechanism of style and character, the first providing an indirect gloss of attitude, the second providing the system of ethical ambiguities which surround and eventually overwhelm the hero. The book opens with a style suitable to the idyllic setting of Saddle Meadows, the sphere of light and love from which Pierre will descend to darkness and hate. "Endless is the account of Love," warbles the narrator: "Time and space can not contain Love's story. All things that are sweet to see, or taste, or feel, or hear, all these things are made by Love. Love made not the Arctic zones, but Love is ever reclaiming them. Say, are not the fierce things of this earth daily, hourly going out? Where now are your wolves of Britain? Where in Virginia now, find you the panther and the pard? Oh, Love is busy everywhere" (p. 38).

The voice here resembles Taji's Emersonian babble when he rhapsodizes over the sunny, shark-filled Pacific, or Ishmael, squeezing himself into the very pulp of philanthropy. It is a facetious, even sarcastic, voice and contrasts with the dark, swirling rhetoric with which Pierre's later descent is described: "Now indeed did all the fiery floods in the *Inferno,* and all the rolling gloom in *Hamlet* suffocate him at once in flame and smoke" (p. 201). This last is the Melvillean grand style, a theatrical rodomontade intended to convey the momentousness of events, whereas the first is the lush, fatuous manner he adopts when he wishes to convey the folly of universal philanthropy. As Pierre sheds his early idealism, the style (like an orchestra in the pit) changes its tone, from scornful schmaltz to symphonic thunder. From opulent, mocking tones, through manifold changes, it reaches a final sympathy with the hero-victim, abandoning off-key praise of love for a style suited to the "dark, mad mystery in some human hearts" (p. 212).

This facetious manner is not entirely abandoned, however, but in the later episodes it is aimed chiefly at the hypocritical world which the hero encounters. Instead of being lush and fatuous, the style takes on a dry, acerb quality, reminiscent of the complex sarcasm of the eighteenth century. This is particularly true of the mock-Chesterfield prose used in the digression on the manipulation of enemies, the ironic exposition of the view that "foes are far more desirable than friends; for who would hunt and kill his own faithful affectionate dog for the sake of his skin? and is a dog's skin as valuable as a tiger's? Cases there are where it becomes soberly advisable, by direct arts to convert some well-wishers into foes. It is false that in point of policy a man should never make enemies. As well-wishers some men may not only be nugatory but positive obstacles in your peculiar plans; but as foes you may subordinately cement them into your general design" (p. 261). This graceful yet biting voice, itself reflecting the "cool, Tuscan policy" that Melville earlier embodied in such characters as Bland, the master-of-arms in *White-Jacket*, presents the reader with a Swiftian paradox of alternatives but no choice.

The knot of style is character, and, as in his earlier novels, Melville provides a paradoxical noose of opposing types. The fatuousness of the opening passages has as its equivalent the Reverend Falsgrave, a masterful caricature of smug, circumlocuting priesthood. Melville's analogy for this "fine, silver-keyed person" is the flute: not only Falsgrave's voice "singularly mild [and] flute-like" but his handsome appearance is compared to "a flute to play on in this world," an instrument of policy of which "he was nearly the perfect master." Falsgrave's "graceful motions" have "the undulatoriness of melodious sounds. You almost thought you heard, not saw him." This unsubstantiality provides further ambiguousness, recalling the undulatory vibrations of the serpentlike Bland, for Falsgrave's "most prepossessing form . . . lost nothing by the character of his manners, which were polished and un-obtrusive, but peculiarly insinuating, without the least appearance of craftiness or affectation" (p. 115). The word "appearance," strong because weak, asserts through denial and is enhanced by the rhythmic counterpoint of diction, in which "prepossessing," "polished," "unobtrusive," are balanced by "insinuating," "crafti-ness," "affectation." The effect is like those bizarre pictures, which, as the viewer changes his position, undergo a strategic metamorphosis, "so that a second face, and a third face, and a fourth face peep . . . from within."

Falsgrave's unsubstantialness is emphasized by his time of life, the penumbral years between youth and middle age, when char-acter has an indefinable quality: "Youth has not yet completely gone with its beauty, grace and strength; nor has age at all come with its decrepitudes; though the finest undrossed parts of it—its mildness and its wisdom—have gone on before, as decorous chamberlains precede the sedan of some crutched king" (p. 116). Although darkened by the image of gouty, vice-ridden old age, the portrait of Falsgrave is intended to be taken as one of sweetness and light, and so intense is the glow from his nimbus that it is impossible to discern a single definite feature. The reader has no idea at all what Falsgrave looks like—he is all halo and music, light and sound.

Mistaking this snowy, amorphous confection for "open benevo-lence and beaming excellent-heartedness," Pierre turns to Fals-grave for advice, but to his unintentional challenge, "Thou art a man of God, sir, I believe," the priest can only stammer, "I? I? I? upon my word, Mr. Glendinning!" (p. 192). For priest is also politician, "a shrewd, benevolent-minded man," who, when "placed between opposite opinions—merely opinions—with a full, and doubly-differing persuasion in himself, still refrains from uttering it, because of an irresistible dislike to manifesting an absolute dissent from the honest convictions of any person, whom he both socially and morally esteems" (p. 120). There is benevolence not in Falsgrave's heart but only in his mind, and his moral estimate waits upon a social appraisal.

The most disagreeable thing about Falsgrave is not his relativism but his opportunistic exercise of it. His artful equivocation is an instrument to be played on in the face of a beastly dilemma, the horns of which might cause him some social discomfort. A politic priest, whose music is patently "of this world," Falsgrave speaks in nothing but preambles and proems—his conversation, like his person, substanceless. In him is met, not the emblematic serpent and dove recommended to the apostles—contained in the brooch hung round his neck to be "sometimes worn on secular occasions"—but rather that union which usually occurs when serpent and dove "unite" in nature: "Unavoidably entangled by all fleshly alliances, [he] can not move with godly freedom in a world of benefices" (p. 193). When confronted by the demands of Christly Pierre, Falsgrave, like the archetypal politician, Pilate, can only ask "What is Truth?" —an equivocation, not a question. As Pierre himself is eventually to discover, only gods can move with "godly freedom."

The idea of Pontius Pilate is a shaping force in much of Melville's later fiction, part of his satiric exploitation of the inutility of the Christian ethic, a historical, physical correlative for the diagrammatic relativity of truth. Falsgrave shares the Roman governor's attitude, but it is the figure of Plotinus Plinlimmon (who shares his initials) that epitomizes the idea of Pilate in *Pierre*. As Falsgrave's shallow hypocrisy typifies the world which Pierre abandons, the complex, evasive Plinlimmon is symbolic of the world which he enters, a labyrinthine, bewildering terrain of ethical considerations which baffles the absolute idealism of Pierre's initial quest. Of a piece with that terrain is Plinlimmon's "sleazy, paper-rag" pamphlet, "Chronometricals and Horologicals," a relativistic treatise on the impracticality of heavenly truth, which uses as its central conceit the difference between Greenwich (chronometrical and absolute) time and local (horological and relative) time. The burden of the pamphlet states one of Melville's favorite themes, that Christ is not of this earth, nor are his ethics (being absolute), but it goes beyond this relativistic stand to promise a median ethic, a "practical virtue" and a "virtuous expediency," to "lay down . . . what the best mortal men do daily practice; and what all really wicked men are very far removed from." But the pamphlet breaks off here with an inconclusive "if" (pp. 252–53).

What Plinlimmon's system might be is suggested by the life led by the philosopher himself, who has withdrawn from life to dwell alone in a tower. Where the priest-politician shuns the extremes of idealism, the philosopher seems to scorn them, though the narrator points out that Plinlimmon's disdain may be Pierre's subjective reaction to the "blue-eyed, mystic-mild face in the old gray tower." Plinlimmon's face, like Falsgrave's, is pleasant enough and expresses a "cheerful content," but the narrator observes that "cheerful is the adjective, for it was the contrary of gloom; content—perhaps acquiescence—is the substantive, for it was not Happiness or Delight." Beyond (or beneath) the cheerful contentment, moreover, there remains "something latently visible in him which repelled." As with Falsgrave, "that something may best be characterized as non-Benevolence. Non-Benevolence seems the best word, for it was neither Malice nor Ill-will; but something passive" (p. 341).

Plinlimmon is another version of relativistic evasion, who prefers to play his flute for his own entertainment instead of circulating in the world. He is pure intellect, all "head," and his heart has atrophied. Whereas Falsgrave is portrayed in terms of music and light, and is, for all his plumpness, nearly invisible, Plinlimmon's features are clearly, if emblematically, sketched. Further, whereas Falsgrave is passing from youth to age, Plinlimmon seems a mixture of both, a blend of contrast reflecting his philosophy, and producing an "inscrutable atmosphere": "Though the brow and the beard, and the steadiness of the head and settledness of the step indicated mature age, yet the blue, bright, but still quiescent eye offered a very striking contrast" (p. 341). So inscrutable seems Plinlimmon to Pierre that even his face appears to be part of a

disguise. Like Moby Dick, Plinlimmon is a sphinx, and only a
simpleton like Charlie Millthorpe could think that he has "wound
himself into Plotinus." A profounder version of nonbenevolence
than Falsgrave, the philosopher presents a baffling, ambiguous
front to the world, protecting himself from its inquiring nose.
Though he is free from the taint of political opportunism, his
chilly isolation damns him. Had he a heart (evidenced by a
family, a hearth, a home), Plinlimmon's withdrawal into a Bur-
tonian cloister might be somewhat mitigated, but to withdraw
from human affection is in effect to die.

Contrasting portraits of nonbenevolent relativism, the philosopher and the priest at once baffle and define Pierre's idealism.
Confronted first by equivocal benevolence, then by inscrutable
nonbenevolence, Pierre's own natural benevolence (itself diluted
by a dubious mixture of idealism and lust) soon perishes. The
paradox is that both the priest and the philosopher are, within the
context of their limited aims, perfectly *right,* whereas Pierre, given
the world as it is, is wrong. Falsgrave has attained a position of
worldly respect and security by maintaining a carefully benevolent
eye on the main chance, and Plinlimmon remains withdrawn and
yet respected within his tower. Both have come to terms with the
relativity of earthly conditions by adopting expedient, evasive
tactics—the one as a politic priest, the other as a priestly philosopher. But Pierre, scorning all equivocation, becomes strangled by
the noose of equivalents.

The hangman is neither priest nor philosopher but is Pierre's
dandified cousin Glen Stanly, who betrays him at a significant
juncture and sees to it that his fall is complete. Glen, who pre-
tends friendship only to betray, is Judas to Pierre's Christ, and like
the other ambiguous characters who surround the hero, is depicted
in contrasting terms: "To quit the mere surface of the deportment
of Glen, and penetrate beneath its brocaded vesture; there Pierre
sometimes seemed to see the long-lurking and yet unhealed wound
of all a rejected lover's most rankling detestation of a supplanting
rival. . . . For the deeper that some men feel a secret and

poignant feeling, the higher they pile the belying surfaces" (p. 264). Surrounded by ambivalent, equivocal characters, the openly idealistic Pierre is at a disadvantage: "All round and round does the world lie as in a sharp-shooter's ambush, to pick off the beautiful illusions of youth, by the pitiless cracking rifles of the realities of the age" (p. 256). But what finally puts an end to his quest (and his life) is neither priest nor philosopher, neither Pilate nor Judas, but the puzzling contradictions contained in the two Marys who attend him throughout—the Magdalen-like Isabel and the Virgin-like Lucy.

III

Lucy and Isabel are romantic stereotypes (Ophelia and Lamia), but Melville uses them to create a baffling juxtaposition of values that further complicates the ambiguities surrounding the hero. Lucy, whose name suggests light and recalls the pastoral maiden of Wordsworth's poems, is identified with the garden loveliness of Saddle Meadows, the Eden of Pierre's youth—a "green and golden world" of "wonderful and indescribable repose" (p. 1). But from the first this dreamlike state is haunted by a succuba, a "dark-eyed, lustrous, imploring, mournful face" that provides "an ill-matched pendant . . . to that other countenance of sweet Lucy" (pp. 42, 47). Like the opposing whale heads hauled aboard the *Pequod*, the faces of dark Isabel and fair Lucy provide a sort of balance, the sort that baffles and finally maddens the absolute idealism of Pierre.

As Plinlimmon's heartless mind is offset by Charlie Millthorpe's mindless heart, so Lucy's openness is balanced by Isabel's mystery. Lucy is at one with the spirit of Saddle Meadows: she is dressed in the colors of "the heavens," and her "golden hair" is matched by the "golden hills" surrounding that "golden world" of love and light, "a flawless, speckless, fleckless, beautiful world throughout" (pp. 37, 70). But Lucy's beauty, like her world, partakes of "the inevitable evanescence of all earthly loveliness," while the mysterious Isabel, "beautiful in soul as well as body," seems "mysteriously exempt from the incantations of decay" (p. 165). In contrast to Lucy, Isabel is mysterious, secretive, associated with darkness (her hair and her home deep within a gothic forest), and where Lucy's appeal is temporal, earthly, Isabel seems to express "the unsuppressible and unmistakable cry of the godhead through her soul, commanding Pierre to fly to her, and do his highest and most glorious duty in the world" (p. 204).

Lucy stands for the present moment, for earthly contentment and well-being, but Isabel represents some transcendent state, her dark beauty revealing "glimpses of some fearful gospel" (p. 49). Her face is a study in contradictions, containing suggestions of both misery and beauty, and seems to Pierre the mirror of the darkness of truth, the suffering that is wisdom. Pierre's "sublime intuitiveness" elevates Isabel's "meaning" to "the sun-like glories of god-like truth and virtue; which though ever obscured by the dense fogs of earth, still shall shine eventually in unclouded radiance, casting illustrative light upon the sapphire throne of God" (p. 131). Like the lush prose used to describe the atmosphere of Saddle Meadows, this rodomontade is suspect because of its use of hyperbole. As Pierre is soon to discover, the mysterious Isabel is as much a daughter of earth as the open, ingenuous Lucy—if not more so.

Faced with the decision "Lucy or God?", the idealistic Pierre can make only one choice, and in doing so he plays out his role of "Enthusiast to Duty," reliving the renunciation by "the heaven-begotten Christ" of mortal considerations (p. 125). But in his decision to redeem Mary-the-sinner, he does harm to Mary-the-saint: "As in his own conscious determinations, the mournful Isabel was being snatched from her captivity of world-wide abandonment; so, deeper down in the more secret chambers of his unsuspecting soul, the smiling Lucy, now as dead and ashy pale, was being bound a ransom for Isabel's salvation" (p. 124). For in obeying his Christ-like feelings, Pierre puts aside the common feelings of humanity, and in becoming a hero, he loses his heart—

like Taji and Ahab before him, he must renounce his common brotherhood with men in order to break through the worldly circle. To become a chronometrical Christ, Melville intimates, is to become a horological Satan.

The priest, the philosopher, Lucy and Isabel—each contributes to the system of balances, "awfully symmetrical and reciprocal," which characterizes the ironic diagram in *Pierre,* at once qualify- ing the hero's idealism and imprisoning him at the center of ethical ambiguity. Truth, warns the ubiquitous narrator, is a peculiar guide, leading the quester into "Hyperborean regions," where "all objects are seen in a dubious, uncertain, and refracting light," a twilight zone where "the most immemorially admitted maxims of men begin to slide and fluctuate, and finally become wholly inverted" (p. 194). Like lost Arctic explorers, wandering through treacherous waters toward the ultimate pole, the truth-led soul often "entirely loses the directing compass of his mind," for at the center of ambiguity, as at the Pole, "the needle indifferently respects all points of the horizon alike." All points are equidistant from the center of a circle.

At first Pierre seems to be between the traditional angels, the good angel who recommends duty and "holds happiness indiffer- ent" and the bad angel who tells him to shun duty "and be happy" (p. 73). Lucy, who seems the golden prototype of the good angel, stands for earthly happiness—which is "bad"—while Isabel, her dark antithesis, stands for heavenly indifference to earthly joy—which is "good." And yet, even as he stands between them, Pierre detects a shade of mournfulness reflected in Lucy's before-happy eyes, and it is not long after he has chosen Isabel that Pierre discovers that his idealistic love for his "sister" threatens to turn into something more earthly. And at the point when he realizes his enthusiastic resolve has been inspired by "womanly beauty" as much as by heavenly truth, the roles of good and bad angels are reversed: Lucy becomes "good" once again, Isabel "bad." Having become saintly through suffering, Lucy comes to the city to share Pierre's apartment with Isabel, and her presence casts further doubt on the hero's already wavering resolve. For in this strange arrangement, it is now Lucy who is the suffering innocent, while Isabel takes on the role of Pierre's proud and jealous mother (who had earlier played at being Pierre's "sister"): "She shall not come! 'Twere a foul blot on thee and me. She shall not come! One look from me shall murder her, Pierre!" Isabel, once the humble outcast, now (in sinning) becomes the defender of social appearances: "Doth not the world know me for thy wife?" (p. 368).

As worldly wife, Isabel loses her former allure. Her darkness, instead of remaining mysterious, suggests the sullen gloom of envy, and her jealous possessiveness dispels the romantic mistiness and unearthly charm with which she was earlier surrounded. While Lucy pities Pierre "with unspeakable longings of some unfathomable emotion," Isabel evinces a more easily defined passion: " 'I would go blind for thee, Pierre; here, take out these eyes, and use them for glasses.' So saying she looked with a strange momentary haughtiness and defiance at Lucy" (p. 411). These reversals, combined with Pierre's increasing doubts about the "entire sum and substance of all possible, rakable, downright presumptive evidence" backing Isabel's claims, eventually result in the hero's final act of self-destruction and his despairing dismissal of both women: "Away!—Good Angel and Bad Angel both!—For Pierre is neuter now!" (pp. 416, 425).

IV

From the outset, Pierre's enthusiasm is qualified by his own doubts "as to the ultimate utilitarian advisability of the enthusiast resolution that was his" (p. 131), a sequence of "insinuating misgivings" which has as its backdrop the "chair portrait" of his father. Serving much the same purpose as the doubloon in *Moby-Dick*, it is Isabel's talisman, supporting her shadowy claim while mocking Pierre's idealistic championing of it and her. The chair portrait is a Claudius, a smiling, lecherous satyr, whose incarnation in Isabel kills the Hyperion in the portrait owned by Pierre's proud mother, the socially proper gentleman of Pierre's inner temple—much as Isabel's advent nearly kills the Ophelia-like Lucy. In the chair painting, the image of his fleshy father and the image of the unearthly Isabel "most magically . . . coincide; the merriness of the one not inharmonious with the mournfulness of the other, but by some ineffable correlativeness, they reciprocally identified each other, and, as it were, melted into each other, and . . . interpenetratingly united, presented lineaments of an added supernaturalness" (p. 100). The metaphorical implication is surely incestuous, imaging the desires which Pierre (son of Pierre) has towards Isabel (imputed daughter of Pierre), which are a subversion of the Platonic feelings he has had towards the sacred memory of his father and the brotherly (but quasi-lover) attitude with which he has regarded his mother.

This incestuous weaving of circumstances (like the hermaphroditic ocean in *Moby-Dick*) traps Pierre in a web of conflicting emotions, but by degrees he comes to identify the ambiguous smile in the portrait as the mocking grin of Satan, and when he leaves Saddle Meadows, he consigns the smiling villain to flame: "For one swift instant, seen through the flame and smoke, the upwrithing portrait tormentedly stared at him in beseeching horror, and then, wrapped in one broad sheet of oily fire, disappeared forever" (p. 233). But the destruction of the portrait does not remove Pierre's doubts, and when he is confronted by a third, final portrait, the "stranger's head by an unknown hand" which so resembles Isabel as to cast suspicion upon the evidence of the chair portrait, it seems "the resurrection of the one he had burnt" (p. 414).

In the confrontation by Isabel and Pierre of the new portrait, Melville once again provides a diagrammatic tableau. Isabel regards the picture as perhaps another portrait of her father, while Pierre, ignorant of her thoughts, sees it as evidence countering the testimony of the burnt portrait. Each, at the same time, expects the other to share his own reflections. Lucy, during this episode, stands facing another portrait, which hangs on the opposite wall of the gallery, a copy of "that sweetest, most touching, but most awful of all feminine heads," Guido's portrait of Beatrice Cenci. The "wonderfulness" of the portrait consists in the contrast between "so sweetly and seraphically *blonde* a being" and the "black crape of the two most horrible crimes (of one of which she is the object, and of the other the agent) possibly to civilized humanity —incest and parricide" (pp. 413–14), crimes of which Pierre himself is presumably guilty also, having slept with his "sister" and "killed" his mother.

In this emblematic tableau, which corresponds to the denouement of a conventional novel, the ambiguities of the plot are not unraveled (we never do learn whether Isabel is Pierre's sister) but rather are drawn into an even tighter knot. The contrast is between innocent-appearing guilt (confronted by innocence) and tragic darkness (confronted by guilt), not so much final balance as a token of the unsolvable problem of existence, the unmatched parts which make any resolution impossible. Like gods of a sort, the two portraits hang above the crowd, "and, from the opposite walls, exactly faced each other; so that in secret they seemed pantomimically talking over and across the heads of the living spectators below" (p. 414). By confronting the reader (not Pierre, who does not see the Cenci portrait) with this contrast, and by expressing it through still another contrast—the world of art juxtaposed with the world of living people, itself really a world of art— Melville repeats the implications of the "Chronometricals and Horologicals" digression, thrusting the "if" forward with a challenge to "Undo it, cut it, quick." The final sum, as in *Moby-Dick,* is a spreading circle.

By structuring this diagram of opposed conditions, a mechanism of antitheses which never cease to cancel each other, Melville at once reveals the fallaciousness of Pierre's idealism (without canceling its nobility) and strikes out at the artificial structure of conventional novels, "their false, inverted attempts at systematizing eternally unsystemizable elements; their audacious, intermeddling impotency, in trying to unravel, and spread out, and classify, the more thin than gossamer threads which make up the complex web of life" (pp. 165–66). Through the insights and blindness of his hero, the one dearly bought, the other fatal, Melville demonstrates that human life comes from that "which all men are agreed to call by the name of *God*; and that it partakes of the unravelable inscrutableness of God." Life does not always end with wedding bells, gloom does not always burst into gladness, and "the profounder emanations of the human mind, intended to illustrate all that can be humanly known of human life; these never unravel their own intricacies, and have no proper endings; but in imperfect, unanticipated, and disappointing sequels (as mutilated stumps), hurry to abrupt intermergings with the eternal tides of time and fate" (p. 166). It is this view of life and art that results in the "ambiguities" of *Pierre*, the diagram of antitheses that dooms the enthusiast quester after truth to dash himself "in blind fury and swift madness against the wall, and [fall] dabbling in the vomit of his loathed identity" (p. 201).

Chapter Seven

Prisoners of the Circle:
Melville's Short Stories

In a round world, where the voyage out necessarily becomes homeward bound, where one man's East is another's West, where a straight line exists only in the mind, it is "easy for man to think like a hero; but hard for man to act like one" (*P*, p. 200). Absolute convictions are one thing, absolute action is another, and all of Melville's questers either lose their convictions or die in the attempt to prove them valid. And from Taji's Byronic plunge into the infinite, to Ahab's sudden strangulation, to Pierre's sordid suicide, the manner of the quester's death seems to increasingly blunt his heroic stature. For Pierre, especially, who dies in the realization that his is an "untimely, timely end," that his "Life's last chapter" is stitched in the middle of a book without a sequel, a book which remains "ambiguous still," heroism seems a quixotic plight at best (p. 424).

Pierre, surrounded still by his ambiguous angels, dies in prison, a setting appropriate to his isolated, outlaw self, and one which accentuates the diminishing stature of Melville's heroes: "The cumbersome stone ceiling almost rested on his brow; so that the long tiers of massive cell-galleries above seemed partly piled on him" (p. 424). Prisons, real or metaphorical, are an important motif throughout Melville's early work—from Tommo's captivity at the hands of the Typees, to the incarcerated king, Donjalolo, to the floating "state prison" in *White-Jacket*—and in each instance they are used to emphasize some human inadequacy of perception or movement. In the short stories which followed the writing of *Pierre*, Melville further expanded this motif, not only by continuing to create "real" prisoners—Bartleby and Benito Cereno—but by drastically reducing the terrain within which his questers operate: a lawyer's office, the decks of a slaver, a New England paper mill. Unlike Taji and Ahab, who hurl themselves across a cosmos, or even Pierre, who has a metropolis to baffle him, the questers of Melville's short stories have literally no place to go. Their quests, correspondingly, are not plunges into mystery, but mere wavering, often bewildered, advances and retreats, attempts to come to terms with a situation beyond their limited understanding. None of them corresponds to the conventional idea of "hero."

Even the style of Melville's stories is affected by the conceptual change, for the rhetoric and rodomontade of the dark romances is replaced by a range of ironic voices, varying from the obtuse, genial persona of "Bartleby" to the sardonic, third-person intelligence which arranges events in "Benito Cereno," each signifying a still further remove from sympathy with the baffled quester. It is true that these changes, all of which relate to a decrease in the kinetic element and a corresponding increase in stasis, may be attributed to the aesthetic limitations of the short story, where concentration of character and event forbids the epic scope of the earlier works. But anyone familiar with the short stories of Melville's contemporaries—even the intensely concentric Poe could set a "Maelstrom" in motion—knows that dynamic action was not limited to the Gothic romance, but was equally characteristic of the "tales" so popular at that time and for many years to come.

It was not so much that the short story form put restrictions on Melville's art, but rather that he abandoned the available form as inadequate for his purpose. Like Poe and Hawthorne, he found the loose, melodramatic tale to be an insufficient vehicle for complexity, its coarse, rambling structure and simplistic emphasis on action unsuitable for nuances of psychological or philosophical implication. Like many of his more popular contemporaries, Melville could have gone on to write endless, inferior versions of "The Town-Ho's Story," but he chose rather to follow the example of Poe and Hawthorne. Indeed, to move from Melville's first experiment in short fiction—the conventional, magazinish "Fragment"—to "The Town-Ho's Story," and on to the terse complexities of "Benito Cereno," is virtually to trace the history of the short story in America.

But what is more important—in Melville's short stories we can also trace the development of his creative consciousness, from the crude romanticism which was satisfied with the simple implications of melodramatic opposition to the more sophisticated state of mind which finds its best expression in total ambiguity. Quest becomes encounter, the basis of the modern story, and, as in modern short fiction, in the world of Melville's stories nothing is known for certain, communication is impossible, and promised relationships never are fulfilled. It is not coincidental that Poe, who invented the modern short story, also invented the detective story, and we may judge the relative modernity of Melville's fiction by the fact that his mysteries, unlike Poe's, are never solved.

Tourists of a sort, Melville's questers in his short stories are also a species of imperfect detective. "The Piazza," written as a thematic prelude to a collection of his best short stories, is Melville's own gloss on their collective implications, and the quester there is a victim of his preconceptions, who stumbles into truth in spite of himself. Each of his other stories, in its way, is also a study in faulty perception, the quester in each a blundering searcher after a mistaken goal, a detective shadowing the wrong man. And in one of the last sketches written during this period, "I and My Chimney," Melville carried the diminishment of his quest structure even further. The narrator of this story is not a baffled quester but rather identifies himself with the object of another's quest. By a process of allusion and metaphor, the chimney of the story becomes at once the narrator's alter ego and a symbol (like the Whale) of the All that is best left undisturbed. His wife, a vain,

industrious woman who is a comic counterpart of Ahab, wants to
tunnel through the chimney in search of a rumored treasure, but
to do so, the narrator suggests, would bring the whole house
tumbling down. Like "The Piazza," the sketch ends with the
recommendation that things should be accepted for what they are,
but the shift of point of view suggests a subtle but significant
change in attitude, a still further remove from empathic identification with the quester. Henceforth Melville's writings become a
version of "chimney" themselves, mysteries which baffle the industrious miners who wish to abstract from them some absolute
significance.

II

Melville's short stories are evidence that as the strength of the
linear element in his diagram declines, the complexity of the circular aspect increases. The pattern of the defeated quest remains
constant, but the emphasis is on the conditions which make success impossible, not on the foolish nobility of the attempt. The
terms of this emphasis are best demonstrated by a study of a letter
which Melville wrote to Hawthorne shortly after he had finished
Pierre but presumably before he began work on his first short
story, "Bartleby." In this letter he outlined an anecdote which he
thought the other writer might work up into a story, and in so
doing he in effect created his own fiction, or at least the bones of
one. A "skeleton," Melville called it, since it lacked the "fulness &
veins & beauty" of a finished narrative. Not only does the letter
reveal the associationist method by which Melville built up the
polarities of his ironic diagrams, but its skeletal condition enables
us to see the thematic patterns so often obscured by indirection in
his finished work.

The story of "Agatha," as outlined to Hawthorne by Melville, is
little more than a structure of paradoxes, adding up to a static
configuration of ironic contrasts. Typically, the action of the story
is limited to the heroine's patient waiting for her sailor husband's

return, "instinct with significance" for Melville, since it typified
"the great patience, & endurance, & resignedness of the women of
[Nantucket] island in submitting so uncomplainingly to the long,
long abscences [sic] of their sailor husbands" (L, pp. 153–54).
Even the storm which casts Agatha's future husband onto Nantucket is ignored in Melville's letter for the sake of the ironic
foreshadowings which are to precede it, the "calm . . . thrown
forth to lead the whole." And the denouncement, in which Agatha
discovers that her husband is not dead but has merely deserted her
for another woman, is scarcely treated at all, though the aftermath
of this discovery is the burden of the anecdote upon which Melville based his letter.

From the beginning, Melville is chiefly concerned with the
paradoxes within which Agatha is held. He first describes his
heroine lying on the brow of a cliff on a "mild & warm" afternoon,
as "the sea with an air of solemn deliberation, with an elaborate
deliberation, ceremoniously rolls upon the beach. The air is sup-
pressedly charged with the sounds of long lines of surf." The prose
here is concerned with contrast, between the mild air and the
deliberate (fated) movement of the ocean, a combination of mildness and threat which Melville used in "The Symphony" chapter
of Moby-Dick. An added note of threat is given in the observation
that the "continual assaults" of the sea on the land "[have] en-
croached also upon that part where [Agatha's] dwelling-house
stands near the light-house."

Like Ahab, Agatha is "filled with meditations" as she "gazes out
seaward," but her thoughts are not revealed. We only know that
she notices a "handful of cloud on the horizon, presaging a storm
tho' all this quietude." The cloud darkens the initial contrast
further, leading to Agatha's sudden awareness of

the long shadow of the cliff cast upon the beach 100 feet beneath her;
and now she notes a shadow moving along the shadow. It is cast by
a sheep from the pasture. It had advanced to the very edge of the
cliff, & is sending a mild innocent glance far out upon the water.
Here, in strange & beautiful contrast, we have the innocence of the

land placidly eyeing the malignity of the sea. (All this having poetic
reference to Agatha & her sea-lover, who is coming in the storm: the
storm carries her lover to her; she catches a dim distant glimpse of his
ship ere quitting the cliff).

(L, p. 156)

The phrase, "poetic reference," is apt, for Melville's method is
animated by a coupling instinct. The sheep and Agatha, the two
shadows on the beach, the conventional calmness preceding a
storm, are all held together in a pattern of shared implications,
paradoxical variations on the themes of innocence and malignity—
an ominous prelude to the ensuing story.

Having framed the initial antithesis, Melville invents a series of
ancillary ironies: Agatha has earlier determined never to marry a
sailor, "which resolve in her, however, is afterwards overbourne by
the omnipotence of Love." Her sea-lover (whom she has helped
rescue—she is his "saviour") overpowers her determination as the
sea overpowers the shore. Her father, too, is "a man of the sea,"
but has been "early driven away from it by repeated disasters."
He keeps a lighthouse, to warn sailors of the perils from which he
has suffered. A human wreck, he has his counterpart in the remains of the ship which brought Agatha's lover. It "becomes
embedded in the sand—after the lapse of some years showing
nothing but the sturdy stem (or, prow-bone) projecting some two
feet at low water. . . . —So that after her husband has disappeared the sad Agatha every day sees this melancholy monument,
with all its remindings." The skeletal prow-bone, jutting from the
sand, suggests the lighthouse kept by Agatha's father, as well as
the post holding the mailbox to which Agatha goes daily for seven-
teen years, hoping for word from her missing husband. This post,
for Melville, is "the *thing*," and stands "at the junction of what we
shall call the Light-House road with [the] Post Rode [*sic*]." As
Agatha's hopes slowly "decay," so does the symbolic post, until it
falls.

The three "posts"—the stem piece, the mail post, and the light-
house—serve as the boundary marks of Agatha's world, and the

bars of her prison as well. Each post contains a meaning of its
own, through association, but all share in the meaning of the
whole, while contributing to it. Taken together, they make up the
diagram of Agatha's condition, the polarities of hope and despair
between which she moves, within which she is held. Her situation
is "significant " because it suggests a truth about the human condition, caught between innocence and malignity, hope and despair, joy and suffering. In such a world there can be no volition,
no freedom, no willed movement—only the restricted pacing of
the prisoner of fate, who has no choice other than patient, humble
endurance.

III

Something of Agatha's stubborn spirit animates Bartleby, the
mysterious scrivener who seems to be waiting silently and patiently for a sign or summons which never arrives, like the dead
letters with which he is associated. From the outset of the story,
when he is set copying documents behind a screen, with his only
window looking out on a blank wall, Bartleby is a prisoner of a
sort, and the preferences which he voices gradually remove him
from the normal activities of life to a real prison, within whose
walls, like Pierre, he dies—a coiled figure of abnegation. Apparently a victim of a world which cannot afford him the understanding he demands, the scrivener is a figurative Christ, whose ways
are not those of men.

Whereas Agatha's long wait is humanly understandable, Bartleby's self-imposed inactivity is not. Like the Whale, he is something of a mystery, a pale specter who writes "palely" in the dim
light of his "blank" window. His eyes—his only distinctive feature
—are "dimly calm" and gray, the penumbral windows of his
shadowy soul. Through his inactivity, Bartleby is a pallid, insub-
stantial challenge to the rational, materialistic basis of his employer's life. And as Ahab pursues the Whale in an attempt to
solve its mystery, the lawyer responds to his scrivener's challenge

by a halting, wavering, ill-defined series of mental circumlocutions, conjectures, hypotheses, and rationalizations. Not so much an advance as a series of sorties and retreats, the lawyer's movements are nonetheless a quest, a journey after meaning which (like Ahab's) reveals more about himself than about the object of his search.

The lawyer is a workaday Christian, a "safe man" who does a "snug business" in a "snug retreat." His ethics parallel the lines in his ledgers, for like Reverend Falsgrave, he has come to terms with the world—and they are profitable terms. The orderliness of his world is suggested by the design of his office: two adjoining apartments, with antipodal windows looking out upon opposing white and black walls, suggesting the cleanly defined ethics of their inhabitant. The office contains a well-balanced system, for the lawyer's two copyists divide their abilities at the meridian, "a good natural arrangement, under the circumstances," a calm, safe, expedient reflection of the planetary order of things.

But like King Donjalolo, the lawyer is a prisoner in his own retreat. Because of his commitment to balance, order, and rational processes, his office is not equipped to handle a case like the mysterious scrivener, the "motionless young man" whose gravity nearly destroys the balanced movements of the lawyer's life. Bartleby demands love that passes all understanding, but what the lawyer cannot understand he only fears. The most he can give is pity, and that is not enough for the scrivener, who continues to put his employer's neat compartmentalizations to the test, confronting his convenient relativism with an absolute demand—a denial that is a cry for recognition. But, like the fly confronted by a windowpane, the lawyer can merely buzz helplessly up and down, imprisoned by the invisible wall of his own inadequacy.

Still, the lawyer is no mere stereotype of cold utilitarianism. Nor does his genial humanity suggest the hypocritical benevolence of Falsgrave. The complexity of this story emerges from his very human self-contradictoriness (Bartleby, though mysterious, is a very simple specter). The lawyer is an average, appetitive man, with human aspirations. He is representative of Adam and Abraham, full of a homely wisdom that has obviously served him well previous to Bartleby's advent. He is a sort of Everyman, and through his vacillations we learn much about the human predicament. Like Pontius Pilate, the lawyer is a type of Roman, and his emblem is the bust of Cicero that stands in his office, for he is a man of the world—rational, vain, good-natured, and above all else a defender of institutions. As fair as he is safe, he does for Bartleby all that is humanly possible.

Bartleby is not Christ, but he is Christly. An outcast and something of a saint, he inspires that "overpowering stinging melancholy," a mood of sadness which Melville seems to have felt was ultimate truth (M, p. 636). But if there is something saintly about Bartleby's otherworldliness, there is something loathsome about it too, and the lawyer's feelings of pity are succeeded by anger and hatred. For to tolerate Bartleby's intolerant refusals is inconceivable in any well-ordered, rational world. His is a "long continued motionlessness" impossible in a world of orderly cycles, an eccentricity that violates the universal concentricity. His demands on the lawyer are unreasonable, even un-right-reasonable, for what can be done for him who prefers to do nothing?

Inevitably, the deaths of messiahs will be brought about by the unheavenly conditions on this earth, for Christianity is unsuitable to the conditions of the workaday world. As a penalty for threatening the worldly order, Bartleby is crucified by it, the victim of a pitying expediency. Rejected at last by virtue of reason, Bartleby becomes the very antithesis of the material world, a coiled circle of emptiness, a cipher which is a token of his mystery. To tolerate him is to bring ridicule and perhaps ruin upon oneself, while to deny him kills him and wrongs that "something superstitious knocking at one's heart," the other unwelcome guest, conscience. In this world, there is no answer to Bartleby's demand, and in denying him the lawyer affirms his own humanity. "Ah, Bartleby!" the lawyer cries, "Ah, humanity!" In his cry the two are linked, Bartleby and mankind, but for Melville the link is paradoxical.

Bartleby, as the scrivener himself makes perfectly clear, has nothing whatsoever to do with humanity. But the lawyer, through his despairing cry, reveals both his ignorance and his own very deep mortality.

IV

The style of "Bartleby," a species of Socratic irony dictated by the created personality of the lawyer, is controlled and uniform, unusual for Melville—who generally preferred a "nimble center" and an "elastic circumference" (P, p. 62), and who was often led by the first-person voice into a display of ventriloquistic versatility. The form best suited to his diagrammatic method was the encyclopedia, which is digressive and discursive by virtue as well as by necessity, and it was with Moby-Dick that he was most successful in bringing about a union of narrative line and organic expansion, a marriage of story and essay. But the encyclopedic form requires great breadth, and in the short stories Melville was forced to either curb his digressive urge or reduce it considerably. As in "Bartleby," complexity is not rendered through great blocks of opposing materials, or through the long dialogues of symposia, but rather through the working out of a comparatively simple exercise in contrasts.

The use of contrasts in Melville's short fiction is most demonstrable in the series of paired sketches, or "diptychs," that he wrote during the same period as his most important stories. "Inverted similitudes," the diptychs are made up of opposing halves, forming a diagram of antitheses, mutually contradictory pairs which add up to a "mystery." Each pair has a narrator, generally presented as a type of "tourist," and hence a quester of a sort. Each half of the diptych is a recounting of a recent trip into an unusual locality or a visit to a singular institution. Ultimately the tourist-quester is baffled by the mystery posed by the contrasting situations he has encountered, so despite a certain emphasis on physical movement,

the absolute implication of traveling, climbing, exploring is ne-
gated by a final balance—a cipher rather than a harmony.

The most memorable of the diptychs (perhaps because of its
sublimation of sexual imagery) is "The Paradise of Bachelors and
the Tartarus of Maids." Both stories concern the adventures of a
wandering salesman, specifically a "seedsman," who recounts a
dinner which he attended in the chambers of the Inner Temple in
London and the peculiar workings of a Tartarean paper mill deep
in a New England valley. The first story is characterized by one of
Melville's inner gardens, the equivalent of the whale circle:
"Going to it, by the usual way, is like stealing from a heated plain
into some cool, deep glen, shady among harboring hills." In the
second sketch, the contrasting setting is a factory deep in a barren,
icy ravine—"a snow-white hamlet amidst the snows."

The first story describes the revels of gay bachelors, "the very
perfection of quiet absorption of good living, good drinking, good
feeling, and good talk," while the second describes the penurious
work of "blank-looking girls, with blank, white folders in their
blank hands, all blankly folding blank paper." Some suggestion of
bias is given by qualifying the "fraternal, household comfort" of
the bachelors by the silent presence of an invalid brother in the
next room, as well as by the admonition that "fine though they be,
bachelors' dinners, like bachelors' lives, can not endure forever,"
the equivalents of the wounded whale which breaks up the bliss
of the whale circle. But the emphasis, as in the case of the two
palaces of Donjalolo, is on the contrast between the selfish, appetitive male principle (here, masturbatory and sterile) and the sere,
pale, and gloomy female principle (virginal and barren). The
dominant symbolism—an inner garden of apparent contentment
contrasted with an immaculate, terrible paleness—is typical of
Melville's "mysteries," and the reaction of the seedsman is baffle-
ment: "All alone with inscrutable nature, I exclaimed—Oh!
Paradise of Bachelors! and oh! Tartarus of Maids!" Like the
well-meaning "Ah!" of the lawyer, the seedsman's "Oh!" is a mere
sound, signifying nothing.

In "The Encantadas," Melville managed a compromise between the "elastic" structures of *Mardi*, *White-Jacket*, and *Moby-Dick*, and the limited, arbitrary divisions of his diptychs. A sort of pocket encyclopedia, "The Encantadas" is a "round," the equivalent of the islands of the Mardian archipelago or the ships that the *Pequod* encounters. Here, however, the linear element is almost entirely missing. The narrator is Salvator R. Tarnmoor, who has once visited the Galapagos and now, a species of tour leader, guides the reader through them and reviews the histories of some of the more notable inhabitants. As in *White-Jacket*, there is hardly any story line, the structure is episodic, and the only thread of continuity is provided by the narrator, who seldom participates himself in the action he is describing.

The implications of the diagrammatic structure here are suggested by two dominant tokens or talismans—Rock Rodondo and the tortoises who are the chief inhabitants of the islands. The Round Rock is a microcosm, the nesting place for all the birds of the region, who divide themselves into "thrones, princedoms, powers, dominating one above another in senatorial array." From the top of the rock, one could get a view of the entire circumference of the chain, but since the rock cannot be climbed, the Enchanted Islands will never (like the Whale) be taken in by a single mortal glance. The rock itself, which is often mistaken for the sail of a ship, shares the illusoriness of the Encantadas, and like them it can never really be known. Surrounded by illusory mists, tricky currents, and baffling perspectives, the islands frustrate the navigator who tries to chart their locations. Like Moby Dick, the islands are a token of the inscrutable wholeness of nature.

The tortoise also is emblematic of nature's wholeness, and his symbolic shell provides the occasion for a quiet little sermon on pessimism and optimism, the balance of which is somewhat weakened by the (implicit) fact that to view the "bright" side of his shell you must turn him over, for his natural position is dark side topmost. Like the Whale, the tortoise is given epic dimen-

sions, his "vast" shell "medallioned and orbed" like "dented and
blistered . . . shields that have breasted a battle," but here again
the tone is mocking, for the tortoise ends up as soup, his shell
serving as a tureen. An unheroic token of the "drudging impulse
to straightforwardness in a belittered world," a cursed victim of "a
penal, or malignant, or perhaps a downright diabolic enchanter,"
the tortoise is compared to those mythical beasts which support the
universe—here plainly a world of unmitigated suffering. Emblematic of futile, painful endeavor, the tortoise is typical of life on
the Enchanted Islands, where existence is reduced by environment
to a stubborn endurance, and where all forward movement ends
finally at a dead wall. His human counterparts are Oberlus and
Hunilla, the Adam and Eve in this fallen world of Tartarean ash,
where "the chief sound of life is a hiss."

Oberlus is a Caliban, damned from the outset by his red-brick,
demonic appearance, and with every act removing himself still
further from the possibility of grace. He is indistinguishable from
the reptiles and rocks of the islands, as grotesque and anachronistic
as the iguana. Even when planting the seeds which are to sustain
his wretched existence, Oberlus' "whole aspect and all his gestures
were so malevolently and uselessly sinister and secret, that he
seemed rather in the act of dropping poison into wells than
potatoes into soil." An epitome of the true Ishmael type, Oberlus is
a lesser Ahab, who yearns for dominion. Like Satan, his besetting
sin is pride of "selfish ambition, or the love of rule for its own
sake."

Like Agatha, Hunilla is an example of human endurance in the
face of intolerable misery. Both she and Oberlus are reduced to
elemental existence, but whereas he strives to prevail over his
environment, to realize his dreams of power, Hunilla merely
clings to the shreds of her former existence, to the mere hope of
hope. Both are prisoners, but while Oberlus seeks actively to
escape (only to end in a real prison), Hunilla waits patiently to be
rescued. One is a victimizer, the other a victim, and though both
are depicted in relation to their wasteland home, Oberlus seems

part of the general malignity that haunts the islands (and is associated with it through bestial imagery), while Hunilla shares with
the tortoises their accursedness and their ability to stubbornly
endure. Not a beast like Oberlus, she is the prey of a "feline Fate,"
who dallies with her "human soul, and by a nameless magic
make[s] it repulse a sane despair with a hope which is but mad."

Like the symbolic reed on which she marks the passage of time,
Hunilla is "long ground between the sea and land, upper and
nether stone," and, caught between these immense contrarities,
like Pip she becomes as indifferent as fate. Since pain is the
condition of Hunilla's existence, she comes to feel that "pain in
other beings, though by love and sympathy made her own, was
unrepiningly to be borne," and as the boat which rescues her
draws away from the desolate, abandoned dogs which were her
only company on the island, she sits "motionless," her face "set in
a stern dusky calm." With all her "lesser heart-strings riven, one
by one," Hunilla emerges from her ordeal with "a heart of yearning in a frame of steel. A heart of earthly yearning, frozen by the
frost which falleth from the sky." A Christ-like victim of inhumanity, she seems no longer a part of mankind, and the figure
on her crucifix has been "worn featureless, like an ancient graven
knocker long plied in vain."

Belonging neither to heaven nor mankind, Hunilla inhabits a
sphere of her own. Even the wretched Oberlus, last seen "burrow-
ing" among mongrels and assassins in a prison cage, remains closer
to common humanity than the saintly Hunilla, "passing into Payta
town, riding upon a small gray ass." The narrator finds some
comfort in her story, for her suffering is testimony to the strength
of humanity, but Hunilla—like that other victim of immensity,
Pip—has long since removed herself from the human bond.
Victim of intolerable mysteries, the silent woman is now a mystery
herself, and like an Egyptian tomb, shows only "her soul's lid, and
the strange cyphers thereon engraved; all within, with pride's
timidity, was withheld." Like Pierre, she has become "neuter," at
one with the universal void.

V

Like "Bartleby" and the diptychs, "Benito Cereno" is a diminished quest. The quester is Captain Delano, another of Melville's tourists whose journey towards truth is so erratic and uncertain that he often seems a victim rather than the master of circumstances. He is nonetheless the agent of exploration—the focus of encounter—and it is through his consciousness that the reader is led into the mystery of the Spanish ship. As in "Bartleby," the center of perception is inadequate, a seafaring version of the lawyer, but here detached from point of view by a delicate operation that allows a third "person" to interpose his wry perspective, shaping Delano's simple optimism into a vehicle of facetiousness. We see things through the American's eyes, but as through spectacles whose rose tints seem somehow discomforting.

The cause of this uneasiness is not revealed until the denouement, for irony of tone depends upon a structural (dramatic) irony, knowledge of the information contained in the concluding deposition. The uninitiated reader may suspect, with Delano, that something is wrong aboard the *San Dominick,* but he is not allowed to perceive anything not revealed to the well-meaning but obtuse protagonist. The method here resembles the detective story, with Delano playing the part of Watson without Holmes, but a significant difference remains. For when the double nature of events is revealed, when the significance of all the clues becomes clear, the decline and death of Benito Cereno remains a mystery, shrouded with the same muteness that characterizes Bartleby and Hunilla. The plot receives a conventional unraveling, but the essential mystery is left unexplained.

Token of this mystery is the melancholy Spaniard, wrapped in his mantle "as if it were a pall," but the sunshiny American is involved in something of a puzzle also. Wrapped not in a pall but in a homespun garment of serenity, "Jack of the Beach" Delano maintains his shore-bound felicity among savages only by clinging to his album of stereotypes, and yet it is his very lack of suspicion which keeps him from a terrible fate. The implication would seem to be that illusion is the safest refuge, yet the very illusions which protect Delano are those which destroyed Don Alexandro and led to Cereno's captivity, suffering, and death. Such is the puzzle of a world whose only consistency is inconsistency, whose brightest light is a midnight gloom.

The deceptiveness of events in "Benito Cereno" is suggested by diction, for the word *seem*, with significant variations (*seemed, seems, seemly*), appears at least fifty-four times, a frequency which abruptly ceases when the counterfeit servant, Babo, reveals his treacherous intent. Similarly, *as if* is used some twenty-seven times, and *appeared* (or *appearance*) fifteen times, ambivalence augmented by *perhaps, apparent, apparently, possibly, evidently, probably, might, no doubt, presume, conjecture, imputed,* and *thought* (in the sense of *conjecture*) at least twenty-six times. In all, there are some one hundred fifteen conjectural expressions in a scant seventy-three pages. Dictated by the narrative mystery, this diction nonetheless hints at the skeptical ontology underlying Melville's quests. These phrases, instruments of style, reflect the lamination of false appearances and unanswerable paradoxes that confound perception and inquiry, a fiction in which things are never as they "seem."

To Delano, things seem well-ordered and naturally benevolent. Leaning over the balcony of the decaying quarter gallery (a scenic device related to the Spanish tragedy of which the captain is still unaware), the American gazes at "the ribbon grass, trailing along the ship's water-line, straight as a border of green box; and parterres of seaweed, broad ovals and crescents, floating nigh and far, with what seemed long formal alleys between, crossing the terraces of swells, and sweeping round as if leading to the grottoes below. And overhanging it all was the balustrade by his arm, which, partly stained with pitch and partly embossed with moss, seemed the charred ruin of some summer-house in a grand garden long running to waste." On one level, the metaphor of the ruined garden is an extension of the idea presented by the crumbling balcony—an emblem of the decaying Spanish nation, whose dying representative is the tragic Benito Cereno. On another level, keyed by the word *seem*, it reflects Delano's habit of putting the most amiable construction on everything he sees, of creating from the wildness of nature a well-ordered, even kindly, pattern. "Naked nature," for him, is "pure tenderness and love," and a Negress whom he spies suckling her "fawn," inspires in him "confidence and ease."

But even as he ruminates on the "formal garden" of seaweed, Delano (much like the transcendental masthead sitter) almost tumbles into the sea—into the depths of the hidden "grottoes"— when the mossy railing on which he leans suddenly gives way. Delano leans too heavily upon appearances of solidity, and it is this which allows him to put a kind interpretation on Cereno's dependency upon his "servant," Babo. Just as balcony railings may usually be counted upon to support a man, so Negroes may be trusted to have a doglike devotion to their masters. Although the American senses a certain disorder on the Spanish ship, he does not suspect the complete misrule which is actually in effect, and he is shielded from the truth by his confidence in the conventional order of things.

He does, however, have his suspicions. His ideas about Spaniards lead him to suspect the gloomy, irritable Don Benito of some foul plot. *Spaniard* means *pirate* in the American's mind, just as *Negro* equals *servant*. But even these suspicions are mollified by Delano's willingness to put a favorable construction on everything that he sees. He is, in many ways, a typical American tourist, "a person of a singularly undistrustful good-nature, not liable, except on extraordinary and repeated incentives, and hardly then, to indulge in personal alarms, any way involving the imputation of malign evil in man." The arrival on board the evil-charged ship of this worldly innocent is heralded by "a white noddy, a strange fowl, so called from its lethargic, somnambulistic character, being frequently caught by hand at sea." As in *Mardi*, though in a different context, the white bird with the bloody feet is a harbinger of disaster.

Like most tourists, Delano is often homesick. His near-fall from the quarter balcony is caused by his eagerness to catch sight of *Rover*, the ship's boat which is filled with associations of home and hearth, a "household boat" whose name suggests both farflung travels and the familiar creature of the hearth, "a Newfoundland dog." The Newfoundland is also used as a simile for Babo, the apparently faithful attendant of Benito Cereno. *Rover*, like the Negro, may be an emblem of home, hearth, and happiness, but on the high seas, where one's front gate opens onto deadly depths, it is a dangerous and illusory memento. Home conventions ("chronometricals") have no validity on strange seas. They seal the eyes of the American sealer to the dangers of the unknown. Here, "away from the influence of land, the leaden ocean seemed laid out and leaded up, its course finished, soul gone, defunct." The sea is not here a formal garden but a coffin, a complement to the funereal furniture of the decaying quarter gallery, whose cabin door is "calked fast like a sarcophagus lid," framed by "a purple-black, tarred-over panel, threshold, and post." A ship of death on a sea of death, the *San Dominick* is carried silently towards "the tranced waters beyond," bearing Captain Delano away from the faithful *Rover*, which yet pursues him, bearing souvenirs of home.

The stasis implied by the leaden ocean and the fixed (relative) distance between the drifting ship (danger) and the pursuing boat (safety) is part of the general lack of movement, the nightmare time which characterizes "Benito Cereno." Physical motion is limited to the American's wanderings about the deck, movement paralleling his thoughts, which are caught in "mazes" of conjecture, held bound by suspicion and reassurance. Held captive by his own limitations, Delano "seemed in some far inland country; prisoner in some deserted château, left to stare at empty grounds, and peer out at vague roads, where never wagon or wayfarer passed." Chained by his mistaken preconceptions, Delano is at once imprisoned and protected, a blessed innocent. Thrown a puzzle-knot, he cannot "cut it."

His antithesis, Don Benito, is also a prisoner, held in the grip of the Negro who seems to support him. Captive of blackness, he is kept deep in the bowels of the "whitewashed monastery" that was once his command. Entombed, he is guarded by Atufal—his mock prisoner—who stands "monumentally fixed at the threshold" of his cabin, "like one of those sculptured porters of black marble guarding the porches of Egyptian tombs." In him is contained the secret of the ship's mystery, as well as the truth of a darker mystery, and Delano, moving through the dimly lighted passage- way that leads to (and from) the cabin, comes as close to the deadly center as he ever gets. For in the blackness of the passage, where all is "eclipsed in sinister muteness and gloom," all events seem "enigmas and contradictions"—the materials of truth. Fright- ened by these shadows, Delano rushes from "darkness to light," from truth to appearances, and finds his beloved *Rover* com- fortably near. He has escaped from the terrible question within the maze, and in fleeing Cereno's prison he has reentered his own.

The rhythm of movement (both physical and psychological) between fear and security (an echo of the situation in *Typee*) is enhanced by patterns of associational imagery and allusion, a species of rhetorical irony. It is by their means that Melville is able to produce the uncanny atmosphere of ambiguous threat that imbues the Spanish ship, at the same time suggesting the vacilla- tions of Delano's mind. The use of imagistic counterpoint is par- ticularly vivid in the episode of Cereno's "shave." Apparently a scene of conventional servitude, it is actually an interlude of tor- ture for the Spaniard, the Negro "slave" serving as his tormentor. The implications of the incident are keyed by the ambivalent articles of furniture with which the cuddy is decorated, like the impromptu barber's chair, "a large, misshapen arm-chair, which, furnished with a rude barber's crotch at the back, working with a screw, seemed some grotesque engine of torment," as well as by the diction used to describe the place: "sharp-ribbed," "Malacca cane," "uncomfortable," "melancholy," "lashed," "hacked," "torn," and "pierced."

The imagery of torment serves to qualify the ensuing episode, with its essay on the natural adaptability of the Negro to the duties of a body servant, where the ironic contrast is unified by the ambiguous names of the servants of Johnson and Byron—"Barber and Fletcher." Cruelest of the ironies is Babo's apparently innocent selection of the Spanish national flag for an apron with which to cover his "master." To Delano, the choice seems further evidence of the Negro's "limited mind," but it is really a sardonic act. Symbolically, the apron summarizes the historical implications of the torture-chamber imagery. Don Benito, the representative of a nation associated with the Inquisition, is here subjected to its indignities himself, draped in a sanbenito made from his own flag and tormented by one who was recently in his power. All of this escapes the American, who nevertheless is made uneasy by "the vagary that in the black he saw a headsman, and in the white a man at the block." But, like all such intimations, this is dismissed as a mere "antic conceit."

Writhing throughout in the apparently tender embrace of his seemingly attentive servant, Benito Cereno is a living reflection of the *San Dominick*'s emblematic stern-piece, on which is seen "a dark satyr in a mask, holding his foot on the prostrate neck of a writhing figure, likewise masked." The masks and the wrestling stance typify the structure (as well as the meaning) of the story, in which tensions emerge from apparent and real oppositions and contrasts. In the end the tensions are broken by the Spaniard's escape from the "dark satyr's" embrace, an act which lifts the seals from the American's eyes, thereby radically accelerating the pace of the story. Further events happen "with such involutions of rapidity, that past, present, and future seemed one." The masks "torn away," the skeleton figurehead "suddenly revealed," there are no more "seems," and the circle of contrasts collapses in a mingling, bloody strife of blacks and whites, a carnal swirl of violence that is accentuated by the lethargy of all preceding events.

As the factitious "order" of the masquerade is succeeded by a bloody flux of reality, this violence in turn is followed by the calm, dispassionate language of the deposition. But the "truth" revealed by the deposition is qualified by the final, unsolved enigma of Benito Cereno's decline and death, a mystery which has as its seal the Spaniard's melancholic silence, muteness matched by Babo's "voiceless end." The motto of the tale would seem to be the set speech which Cereno delivers to Captain Delano: "To such degree may malign machinations and deceptions impose. So far may even the best man err, in judging the conduct of one with the recesses of whose condition he is not acquainted. But you were forced to it; and you were in time undeceived. Would that, in both respects, it was so ever, and with all men." Yet the weight of the declaration does not fall on "undeceived," but on the conditional "would that," implying that Delano's "flash of revelation" is the exception rather than the rule. The silence and darkness shrouding the deaths of Cereno and Babo are the "truth" of man's condition. Silence, not communication, darkness, not light—these are the thresholds of mystery—and the affairs of men are chiefly characterized by isolation, frustration, and truncation. Events in life do not attain the wholeness and perfection of art, "never unravel their own intricacies, and have no proper endings: but in imperfect, unanticipated, and disappointing sequels (as mutilated stumps), hurry to abrupt intermergings with the eternal tides of time and fate." As the onrush of all rivers must terminate in the great planetary rhythm of the ocean, so the endeavor of each man is ultimately absorbed by the wholeness of being, which is given roundness by death. We are all prisoners of the circle.

Chapter Eight

Versions of the Picaresque:
Israel Potter and *The Confidence-Man*

The dominant note in Melville's most ambitious writings through *Pierre* is defiance, expressed through open outrage or through indirect, subversive attacks. In those early writings the linear element also is often strong (*White-Jacket* is the great exception) and is expressive of Melville's personal investment in the fortunes of his quester. But as that investment diminished, as the line of the quest threatened to merge with the static, circular element, a note of acquiescence—a minor theme in the early works—gradually emerged, to dominate in turn the poems and sketches of Melville's years of retirement and solitude. In the final pages of *Israel Potter* are found the first signs of that ultimate mood.

The scarred, worn-out Israel in London is a prefiguration of the weird old men who inhabit Melville's last fiction, a transition between the gnomic Manxman in *Moby-Dick* and the mysterious Dansker of *Billy Budd*. Like Daniel Orme, Israel bears a token of hardship—a crosslike scar—and like the old sailor he seems to have made some sort of peace with existence. If defiant old Ahab recalls Lear on the heath, mild old Israel suggests Lear in prison: "In want and bitterness, pent in, perforce, between dingy walls, he had rural returns of his boyhood's sweeter days among them; and the hardest stones of his solitary heart (made hard by bare

endurance alone) would feel the stir of tender but quenchless
memories, like the grass of deserted flagging, upsprouting through
its closest seams" (p. 217). There are echoes here of Ahab, peer-
ing into a meadowlike ocean just before his final hunt, of Hunilla,
grown hard through endurance, and Bartleby, curled up and
dying on a soft, prison turf. The implicit metaphor of walls and
imprisonment relates Israel Potter to those other prisoners in
Melville's short stories, whose movements are severely limited by
physical or psychological barriers.

Yet *Israel Potter,* with its rambling, disjunct structure, is a
picaresque novel, a genre in which the linear, narrative element
traditionally dominates the structure. Throughout the first two-
thirds of the book action is fast-paced, the narrative is crowded
with adventures, and the reader is swept across America, Europe,
and England—as well as through the course of a man's life—in a
few hours' reading time. The style, suitably, is open and direct, for
the most part without the ironic discursiveness which characterizes
the short stories that were being written during the same period.
But *Omoo* is also a picaresque narrative, and no better register of
the changes in Melville's art and attitude can be found than the
difference between these two books.

Whereas the narrator of the early work is ebullient, rebellious,
foot-loose, traveling wherever his inclinations lead him, Israel is
generally under orders, a soldier of ill fortune, "repeatedly and
rapidly . . . planted, torn up, transplanted, and dropped again,
hither and thither, according as the Supreme Disposer of sailors
and soldiers saw fit to appoint" (p. 111). "Omoo" means "wanderer," but "Israel" connotes the tribe wandering in bondage, and
Israel Potter is the captive not only of the English Egypt but of
poverty and the vagaries of fate as well. His only acts of volition
are his inspired enlistment into the army and his subsequent vol-
unteering for duty aboard the brigantine *Washington.* After that,
taken prisoner by the British ship *Foy* and put on the frigate
Tartar, he begins a long voyage dictated by the whims of fate.
Passed from place to place, acted upon by person after person, he
becomes more important as a device for displaying a panorama of

historical incidents and characters than as a person in his own right.

Unlike Melville's earlier heroes, who are depicted as plunging onward to their destinies, Israel's progress is figured in terms of flight, "tattered coat-tails streaming behind him," a motif signaling his enforced alienation from the society in which he moves. His life is a continual, solitary hegira to nowhere. The kineticism, as in the heroic quests, emerges not from the impress of the quester's will upon events but rather from the pressure of events upon the quester. Israel's quest consists of a wish to return home, but all things act against him, moving him away from the place towards which he yearns—a hapless Ulysses, his onrush is backward, not forward, a tumbling down the stairs of life. "Who are you?" becomes an inquisitional chorus, for Israel becomes many things without becoming anybody: first farmer, then surveyor, pioneer, trapper, trader, sailor, harpooneer, soldier, prisoner, spy, beggar, gardener, brickmaker, chairmender, patriot, alien, immigrant, emigrant, exile, deserter, volunteer—the hero is whirled through a kaleidoscope of costume changes signifying nothing.

Israel's plight is emphasized by contrast. Ben Franklin and John Paul Jones are the antitheses of character which are one aspect of Melville's diagram, planetary antipodes which exemplify the worldly success and dynamism which Israel so sadly lacks. Like Falsgrave and Plotinus Plinlimmon, they are securely anchored in the world, while Israel cannot even manage a fingerhold. And finally, by regarding his hero's plight from a third-person point of view, Melville creates an effect of distance, an ironic bias that diminishes him still further. Though regarded sympathetically, Israel is entirely a plaything of exterior forces, his destiny a demonstration of the miserable lot of common man when he happens to get caught up in the struggle of nations.

II

An episode which typifies Israel's plight is the one in which he finds himself carried by a freak circumstance from the decks of an

American ship to those of an English man-of-war. Clinging to the boom of the enemy vessel, Israel is plucked from the side of John Paul Jones—the only person in the book towards whom he feels a kinship—and is planted in the midst of those whom he most hates. Protected for a time by the darkness of night, Israel can only hope to find himself a billet before daybreak, to become one of the enemy. At first taking heart at the English captain's "shouting-out that half his men were killed," Israel eventually discovers that this was only a tactical deception, that there are no dead men and hence no empty billets. Like White-Jacket, Israel becomes a pariah, a stranger in a strange land, and his search for a billet becomes a parable in which the English ship is a microcosm of society and he a misfit engaged in a search for charity.

Starting in the maintop and ending down in the bilges with the miserable waisters, Israel acts out his eventual descent from an American freeholder to a wretched English beggar. His masquerade is in vain, however, for there is no room for him, or charity either. Then, as dawn comes, his identity is questioned by "an irascible fellow whose stubborn opposition our adventurer had long in vain sought to conciliate" (p. 181). This bearish individual is a shaggy malcontent who has the gift of smelling out the impostor beneath the wool, and, aroused by his grumbling, each of the crew declares that he, in turn, had been "molested by a vagabond claiming fraternity, and seeking to palm himself off upon decent society" (p. 182). Finally, in the gray light of dawn, Israel is recognized as unrecognizable and is made prisoner by his enemies.

Taken before the officer of the deck "as a mysterious culprit," Israel causes much confusion. His presence not being accounted for officially, like Bartleby he threatens the delicate balance of rational (martial) order: "Where did you come from? What's your business? Where are you stationed? What's your name? Who are you, any way? How did you get here? and where are you going?" (p. 182). Unlike Bartleby, Israel is eager to pitch in and work. He entertains no notions of patriotic zeal and wishes only to save his skin by enlisting as a member of the enemy crew. But because he has no former identity, he can have no present position. Like Bartleby, he seems "out of all reason; out of all men's knowledge and memories!" (p. 183). Not being able to account for Israel on any rational basis, the officer of the deck decides that "He must be out of his mind," and Israel (for once seizing an advantage) assumes a madcap air and saves himself. By adapting to the absurdity of the situation, he survives.

If Israel is a hapless Ishmael, an outcast wanderer, his counterpart is the fierce, Ahab-like Ishmael, John Paul Jones, whose "confidential man" he becomes. Jones is "a rather small, elastic, swarthy man, with an aspect as of a disinherited Indian chief in European clothes" (p. 72). His character made up of contrasts between savage and civilized traits, he is a metaphorical half-breed, whose paradoxical character is mirrored in his face: "Hidden power to back unsuspected projects, irradiated his cold white brow, which, owing to the shade of his hat in equatorial climates, had been left surmounting his swarthy face, like the snow topping the Andes" (p. 81), an emblem which he shares with Captain Ahab. Jones is a "combination of apparent incompatabilities," contraries of "regicidal daring" and "octogenarian prudence" (p. 131), whose savagery is mingled with a "dash of pleased coxcombry," and who carries himself with a "rustic, barbaric jauntiness, strangely dashed with a superimposed touch of the Parisian *salon*" (pp. 80, 72). The very model of barbarism, Jones is a literal man of war, his ferocity an implicit answer to the rhetorical question, "Is civilization a thing distinct, or is it an advanced stage of barbarism?" (p. 173).

Jones's silk-enfolded savagery is an emblem of the stealth and cunning which characterize his battle tactics. Half-gentleman, half-wolf, he is a "Coriolanus of the sea," only slightly better than the intriguing Oberlus. "The devil in a Scotch bonnet," Jones glides unseen into enemy harbors, his ship disguised as a merchant-man—"under the coat of a Quaker, concealing the intent of a Turk" (pp. 131, 127). Ahab, too, is a Quaker with a fiery heart, and Jones's hatred of the British is a version of Ahab's hatred of the White Whale. Like Ahab, Jones is a symbol of the country he serves, the renegade, revolutionary America: "Intrepid, unprincipled, reckless, predatory, with boundless ambition, civilized in externals but a savage at heart, America is, or may yet be, the Paul Jones of nations" (p. 158).

Whereas, in Israel, many identities add up to no identity at all, in Jones a paradoxical personality supplies the complexity necessary for survival in a paradoxical world: a coxcomb in Paris, Jones is a savage at sea. His antithesis, Ben Franklin, exists in a more subtle, more complicated world, and whereas Jones is as cunning as a wild Indian, Franklin is portrayed as a veritable Machiavelli, combining traits of slyness and benevolence, a Merlin who issues *Poor Richard's Almanac* from under his philosopher's stone of proverbial common sense. Sage, idol, man of mystery, the "sapient inmate" of the wily world has something benign about him and something devilish, too. Like Oberlus and the Whale, he shows only his back parts to the world, a featureless blank that is for Melville a token (albeit Rabelaisian) of God's indifference to the propositions of mankind.

The God of Melville's fictive world is Jugglarius, a trickster deity, and Franklin is his priest: he appears to give favors but really takes things away, and the floor of his study is so slippery that Israel nearly makes a pratfall entrance. To Israel's bumpkin, Franklin plays the cosmopolitan con man, and although he does not injure his unfortunate countryman, or cozen him for any profit, his reassurances and encouragement of trust in one's fellow man seem somehow hypocritical, seeing that Franklin is the center of a spy ring. His simplicity is that of Socrates, and Israel Potter is not his only victim. Even the complex Jones is a simpleton when he confronts Dr. Franklin.

Whereas in Jones cosmopolitanism is a thin veneer, in Franklin it is the very material of his being. The irony of this contrast is brought out in an interview between the sage and the sailor, in which Franklin's outward simplicity becomes a mirror of the essential innocence of the rakish barbarian. Though Jones is capable of a savage cunning, he is no match for the Tuscan talents of the philosopher-statesman, who condescendingly rubs his knee as if scratching an angry lion behind the ears. In reply to Jones's open, "Thank you for your frankness. . . . Frank myself, I love to deal with a frank man. You, Doctor Franklin, are true and deep, and so you are frank," the sage smiles as if in agreement, but with "a queer incredulity just lurking in the corner of his mouth" (p. 76). Franklin knows that frankness (openness) is never the vehicle of deep truth, and the captain, who should have known better, is lured outside his depth.

Franklin, like the Whale, is a complex, intricate symbol of the labyrinthine world, the domain not of sea monsters but of men. Job's Leviathan gives way to Hobbes's, the small world of affairs, of commerce between members of a society. Franklin is eminently qualified to represent that society, having been "printer, post-master, almanac maker, essayist, chemist, orator, tinker, statesman, humorist, philosopher, parlor man, political economist, professor of housewifery, ambassador, projector, maxim-monger, herb-doctor, wit" (p. 62). He stands for the microcosm with which satire is concerned, the world of petty projects and intrigues, the busy world of business. Franklin, the arch businessman, is a type of Yankee, like Israel a "Jack-of-all-trades." But Franklin's progress in life has been successful, a series of steps upward, while Israel's is a descent. Israel's many changes do not produce wealth and are impelled by need, not ambition. He is not the master of conditions, but the victim (the fool) of them. He is the fool of the world which Franklin represents, and Franklin's puzzle is the enigma of worldly success whose key Israel lacks. Though Israel's journey eventually brings him full round, he returns to America in the rags of a pauper, his estate a "Potter's field" gone to waste.

III

The Confidence-Man is another of Melville's diminished quests, here the search for confidence by a metaphysical conycatcher. Though the confidence man is "a seeker, not a finder," he is the antithesis of Taji, Ahab, and Pierre. His many-sided character is dominated by repeated avowals of optimism—towards nature and mankind—and his stature, like that of the "heroes" of the short fiction, is decidedly unheroic. If in Israel we have a picaro-victim, in the confidence man we have a victimizer, a Jonathan Wild to Israel's Roderick Random. He is an agent of facetiousness, engaged in a foolish quest staged as the instrument of knavery, and, despite his good cheer, he is one of the darkest (in implication) of Melville's questers.

In marked contrast to *Israel Potter*, the movement in *The Confidence-Man* is slow-paced, miniscule, assisted by a self-conscious and heavily ironic style, reminiscent of the balanced periodicity of the eighteenth century, and tending towards a complex, parenthetical manner that suits the obscure aims of the protagonist. There is, strictly speaking, no action, merely a series of conversations that eventually assume the form of a symposium, a round of opinions producing a static pattern of attitudes—another variation on the dialogue "rounds" in *Mardi* and *Moby-Dick*. The book ends with the suggestion that it might be continued, and—like *Moby-Dick*—the structure is such that it could be expanded forever by continued accretion. The action is further slowed by interpolated anecdotes, illustrative parables that enhance the major themes of the book but which do nothing to advance the narrative line. And finally, as if to emphasize the differences between Melville's two attempts at the picaresque novel, the action is strictly limited in time and space: it takes place on the decks of a river boat and within the duration of a day.

Despite these many structural differences, the two novels share at least one important theme. The idea of worldly success dominates the many Socratic dialogues which the confidence man has with the steamboat passengers, and—like Ben Franklin—the confidence man is a man of the world, a creature of many guises who is able to confront each passenger in turn with an argument tailored to his disputant. Apparently inconsistent, the confidence man is actually a miracle of consistency. With his watch set to horological time, his many-sided personality reflects the multi-fariousness of mankind. Like the conversations in which he takes part, he becomes a diagrammatic round himself, assuming the fullness of all humanity.

Unlike Franklin, however, the confidence man is seldom successful. In his quest for confidence he is generally rebuffed by the world, and even when he seems to succeed, the reader is left (like the customer) with an uneasy feeling that the conversion is not permanent. Though his arguments are set to horological time, his quest is absolute and chronometrical and cannot succeed. All his many changes—his masquerade—are in vain, and though he seems to progress (from the sleazy operators he first represents to the gorgeous swindler, Frank Goodman), the progression is illusory. Starting at dawn, he moves into darkness, the gloom which counters his cheery advocacy of benevolence. As the confidence man leads his last victim off into the night, the absolute blackness which he leaves behind him tokens the hollowness of his many arguments for light.

The implication of the progress from dawn to dark and mean-ness to splendor (a counterpoint of philosophical as well as disguise "changes") is suggested by the preludelike outset of the book, in which the main issues and events are prefigured. In the opening pages, a deaf mute appears at sunrise, writing various appeals for charity (Biblical quotations from 1 Corinthians) only to be shoved aside by the callous crowd of passengers. His successor, a noisy Negro beggar, has better luck in gaining the attention (and confidence) of the passengers by playing the clown and catching pennies in his mouth. The meaning of the contrast would appear to be simple: there is no faith on the *Fidèle*. The ship contains a "No Trust" world which has lost the spirit of true charity, and which demands something in return for its money besides love. The pale, flaxen-haired mute, who arrives only to be spurned by the materialistic, carnival crowd, seems the very embodiment of Christianity. He contains the "soft, curled, her-maphroditical" look which Melville associated with Christ, the "feminine . . . submission and endurance, which on all hands it is conceded, form the peculiar practical virtues of his teachings" (*MD*, p. 373). Like Bartleby, he is a creeping Jesus: "As an intruder he came; and an intruder would he be this day" (*M*, p. 628).

However, like Bartleby, the mute is something more than a figuration of Christ. His dumb silence is a token of his helplessness, but it has other meanings as well. If "in silence the child Christ was born into the world," so also are "all profound things and emotions of things . . . preceded and attended by Silence" (*P*, p. 239). Like the beautiful deaf-mute in the "Fragment," or like the silent Whale, the voiceless wonder whose advent sets the narrative in motion speaks volumes to the initiated—he is a threshold of Mystery. Set down among the pilgrim-hunters and the hunter-pilgrims, the effeminate figure of the mute brings to mind Chaucer's pardoner, that prototypal confidence man, a parallel which seems borne out by the subsequent development of the story. The mute is but one form assumed by a protean jackanapes who, like the pardoner, contains limitless possibilities for equivocation and deceit, who bears a Christian message and a Christian demeanor only to prove the inefficacy of Christianity as a workable ethic on earth.

The Christly mute is a blank, an outline to be filled in by a number of tricksters to follow, who will turn his impassive message of charity into a persistent appeal for confidence. That the mute, despite his unlikeness to those who follow him, is one of the gang is hinted both by the metaphysical contingency and by his taking a stand near a placard offering "a reward for the capture of a mysterious imposter, supposed to have recently arrived from the East" (p. 1). When the mute disappears, to be succeeded by a crippled Negro, we are treated to the first of many such changes. "Knotty black fleece" replaces the white "fleecy nap" on the mute's hat, and out of this unholy sacrament, a union of black and white, springs the sequence of tricksters to follow. The contrast of white mute and black chatterbox initiates a pepper-and-salt motif that is maintained throughout the narrative by a suggestive progression of colors.

Thus, the next confidence man, Mr. Ringman (whose name is a cant word for "impostor"), wears a dark mourning suit and a black weed in his hat, but is otherwise white. His white successor wears gray over a white shirt, the quack "Bonesetter" sports a snuff-colored surtout, and the gradual reduction in darkness (not accompanied by any decrease in duplicity—quite the reverse) results in the sartorial splendor of Frank Goodman, the most complex guise of the confidence man, who comes dressed in a coat of many colors. It is he, more than any other, who is an embodiment of the idea that things are never black and white, that the most genial smile may hide a villain, but that a genial villain is a pleasanter companion than a scowling saint.

The ghostly mute is a personification of Scripture, a proponent of charity who is as silent, white, and unresponsive as the page upon which the Word is written. Like that page he is an impersonal statement to be accepted through faith or turned away. The Negro is his antithesis. His name—Black Guinea—suggests that he is an emblem of perverted, counterfeit value, a coin so debased that it has become black and corroded. His talisman is "the old coal-sifter of a tambourine" he carries, a token of the eclipsed sun of truth. With Guinea's appearance, the immaculate Word is henceforth blackened and perverted, debased to the catchword of the crooked operators.

And yet "confidence" (*con-fidens*) contains the idea of charity, and the confidence man's pleas for faith in himself are as futile as the mute's silent scripture. Small wonder that charity is turned aside, if simple trust cannot gain a footing on the slippery decks of the *Fidèle*. The situation is further complicated by the fact that although the confidence man is not "good," neither is he explicitly "bad." Implicitly demonic, misanthropic, cynical, he is avowedly humanitarian and optimistic. He says one thing, is another, and in the long run is both. In him the forces of Christ and the Devil are met, and the union—like the marriage of serpent and dove—is peaceable, even synergistic. Christianity, plainly, makes suckers of us all—those who peddle it as well as those who buy.

This seems to be the implication of the final scene in the book, where events are illuminated by the dim, smoky lamp of the "gentleman's cabin"—a setting reminiscent of the catacombs in which the early Christians hid from persecution. Here, Frank Goodman leads off into darkness a doting old man, a patriarchal, saintly, but obviously senile figure—like the pusillanimous mute, a symbol of dying Christianity. Before he is led off into final darkness, the old man has certain dealings with a strange youth, leopard-toothed, and dressed in colorful rags that resemble "the painted flames in the robes of a victim in *auto-da-fe*" (p. 277). As in "Benito Cereno," the Inquisition imagery is a token of dying institutions, for the flaming boy sells Father Christian a number of "No Trust" items, changing him from a pious Bible reader to an emblem of materialism and empty faith. He is motivated by suspicion, greed, and doubt, those very forces which nourished the Inquisition: faith gone, fear rushes in.

This is the ultimate intimation of the Christ concealed within Satan, the Satan within Christ. Christianity, with all its sweet sounds, bore in its bosom the serpent of self-destruction. On this earth, at least, Christ only prepares the way for anti-Christ, as the mute is the harbinger of Black Guinea. On this earth, it is the last who is most successful, but even he must resort to shabby tricks in order to attract the attention (if not the allegiance) of mankind.

In the end, it is mankind, not the confidence man, who is culpable, for every cycle in the repetitive pattern of duplicity takes its impetus from the folly and greed of the passengers, of which the confidence man is only the index, not the source. "Society his stimulus, loneliness was his lethargy. . . . Left to himself, with none to charm forth his latent lymphatic, he insensibly resumes his original air, a quiescent one, blended of sad humility and demureness" (p. 48). It is from the passenger's hopes and fears that he takes his energy and identity, and the concluding statement, "Something further may follow of this Masquerade," suggests that his character is as infinite in its manifestations (and implications) as "that multiform pilgrim species, man" (p. 8). Everything to all men, he is no man himself. Even his incessant quest for confidence is a figurative rather than a psychological motive.

As one passenger suggests, the confidence man is "A fanatic quack; essentially a fool, though effectively a knave" (p. 101). He is the fool of confidence, as Pierre is the fool of truth. Not only is he pledged to pursue it for its own sake, without apparent profit, but he is further dedicated to pluck out whatever grains of confidence he has managed to sow, almost as if to prove that it is so scarce a seed that he cannot afford to leave it broadcast for long. Having convinced the barber to forswear his "No Trust" sign (a dominant talisman), he saunters away without paying the man, and within moments the sign is back where it belongs.

The story takes place on the first of April, and the traditional trick is to send someone on a fool's errand. When a young clergyman goes in search of Black Guinea's "friends," a one-legged cynic calls it a "wild goose chase," but, shortly afterwards, the clergyman is successful. Ultimately, ironically, it is the quixotic confidence man who is on a wild-goose chase, who runs the errand of a fool. Like the quests of Taji, Ahab, and Pierre, his ends in failure, for the old man he leads off into final darkness is not much of a conquest, nor has the old man, encumbered with the furniture of suspicion, availed himself of much confidence—save in devices dependent upon fear.

IV

Although the episodic structure, the down-river journey, and the presumably inconclusive ending of *The Confidence-Man* would seem to suggest a linear construction, the overtones of the opening and closing scenes suggest that the book, like *Israel Potter*, is a thematic round, an arrangement of forces designed to enhance the futility of the quest for confidence. Starting at dawn with a

Christly mute and ending at midnight with an old Christian and final silence, Melville would seem to be constructing a full circle of metaphysical antitheses. That this is indeed so is suggested by other aspects of structure, like the diagrammatic round (symposium) of conversations, each of which contributes to the physical stasis characteristic of Melville's diagram.

As in *Moby-Dick,* the opposition of line and circle is enhanced by a contrast of styles, here, between the platitudinous rhapsody of the confidence man (equivalent, though antithetical in content, to Ahab's wild rhetoric) and the sly, indirect manner of the narrator, the "third person" who occasionally (like Ishmael) intrudes to comment on matters. With the modesty of a billboard, Frank Goodman advertises himself as "A cosmopolitan, a catholic man; who, being such, ties himself to no narrow tailor or teacher, but federates, in heart as in costume, something of the various gallantries of men under various suns. Oh, one roams not over the gallant globe in vain. Bred by it, is a fraternal and fusing feeling. No man is a stranger" (p. 151). Pursuing sunshine as Ahab pursues darkness, he babbles sentiments like those of Taji or the rhapsodist of the opening pages of *Pierre.*

But, like those earlier paeans of universal benevolence, the confidence man's joyous espousal of mankind has an off-key ring, a facetiousness which is emphasized by the far less easy view of humanity implied in the narrator's digressions. In contrast to the gushing outpour of the cosmopolitan's easy views, the style of the digressions is broken by commas, qualifiers, and parenthetical phrases, a syntactical stuttering which betrays the inherent skepticisms within: "Upon the whole, it might rather be thought, that he, who, in view of its inconsistencies, says of human nature the same that, in view of its contrasts, is said of the divine nature, that it is past finding out, thereby evinces a better appreciation of it than he who, by always representing it in a clear light, leaves it to be inferred that he clearly knows all about it" (p. 77). The idea contained here, like the drift of the cetology chapters, implies that one does indeed "roam over the gallant globe in vain," that all straightforward conclusions are in vain. Mankind (and deity) is no easy matter to define, a difficulty suggested by the mass of subordinate qualifiers and parenthetical interjections which supports the essential sentence, "He who says of human nature the same that is said of divine nature, that it is past finding out, evinces a better appreciation of it than he who infers that he knows all about it." Or, in blunter diction, "He who says of man what is said of God, that He cannot be known, speaks truer than he who says he knows all about him." Like the Whale, man (and God) is multiform and undefinable, and a style proper to this idea is as vague and knotty as the confidence man's is free and easy.

Opposition of styles is reinforced by implications of imagery and allusion. The confidence man, after all, is engaged in what even the most naïve reader would recognize as the form, if not the substance, of a swindling operation, and there are many hints that he is *the* confidence man, a silky Mississippi Mephistopheles: "Then softly sliding nearer, with the softest air, quivering down and looking up, 'could you now, my dear young sir, under such circumstances, by way of experiment, simply have confidence in *me?*'" (p. 30). A third device which counters the smooth-flowing optimism and bustling advance of the confidence man is the use of anecdotes, short interpolations of treachery and betrayal that provide implicit comment on man and nature. Some of these are brief *exempla,* but there are longer inclusions, a total of five bitter tales whose collective moral may be summed up by the barber's sign: "No Trust."

Further opposition is provided by the series of malcontents who confront the confidence man with surly denunciation. The first of these is the "limping, gimlet-eyed, sour-faced" cynic who calls Black Guinea a sham. A one-legged, satiric version of Ahab, who makes "himself miserable for life, either by hating or suspecting everything and everybody" (p. 11), he is dedicated to reducing the world to a hypocritical facade. Though presented with an air of disdain and distaste, on his acid tongue rests the sour kernel of the book: "To where it belongs with your charity! to heaven with it! . . . Here on earth, true charity dotes and false charity plots" (p. 14). It is this civetlike stink of distrust which is seemingly the only protection against the confidence man, who sorrowfully denounces the cynic as "A bad man, a dangerous man; a man to be put down in any Christian community. . . . Ah, we should shut our ears to distrust, and keep them open only for its opposite" (p. 36). His many "Ah's" and "Oh's" are as empty as his easy philanthropy, treacle curdled by the cripple's wormwood of truth —a distillation of Melville's favorite theme, that "Charity is one thing, and truth another." And yet there is no denying the confidence man's premise, for the one-legged cynic has no place in a "Christian community"—his acid wisdom corrodes as well as curdles. Listening to him unwillingly, and cheering a Methodist preacher who denounces him, the passengers nonetheless are stung to distrust by this "Canadian thistle" of misanthropy.

An even more extreme case of the gloom which is proof against the confidence man's blandishments is the dark giant who boards the *Fidèle* at "a houseless landing, scooped, as by a land-slide, out of sombre forests; back through which led a road, the sole one, which, from its narrowness, and its being walled up with story on story of dusk, matted foliage, presented the vista of some cavernous old gorge in a city" (p. 96). Like Enceladus, the "invalid Titan" is of nature, but a creature undreamed of by Shaftesbury, "his beard blackly pendant, like the Carolina-moss, and dank with cypress dew; his countenance tawny and shadowy as an iron-ore country in a clouded day." Bent over under an invisible burden, the mournful giant seems a human counterpart to the enchanted tortoise, a victim of some intolerable curse. Confronted and tormented by the confidence man's claims for a "natural" pain dissuader, the invalid grizzly knocks him down and denounces him for a fraud: "Some pains cannot be eased but by producing insensibility, and cannot be cured but by producing death" (p. 99). The confidence man is left with the final word—"Regardless of decency and lost to humanity"—and though the sentiments ring false, they do point up the fact that the only proof against his wares is absolute rejection of his philanthropic premise.

A less extreme alternative is presented by Pitch, the admirable Missourian, who, though not crippled or under any great psychic burden, is nonetheless a bearish mistruster of Mother Nature. Having long suffered at her hands, Pitch is equally intolerant of the confidence man's faith in "natural" cures, and like the invalid Titan, he is successful in refuting the herb doctor's claims for his pills. But his distrust of human nature earns him a familiar and perhaps deserved rebuff: "Since, for your purpose, you will have neither man nor boy, bond nor free, truly, then some sort of machine for you is all there is left" (p. 128).

Still, Pitch's outbursts against human nature are only a mask. He wants to have confidence in his fellow man, and like Babbalanja is uncomfortable in his unbelief. "Surly-looking as a thunder-cloud with the inkept unrest of unacknowledged conviction" (p. 140), he is discharged of his lightings by the man with the brass plate, who draws him by subtle chains of logic into the open ground of common humanity. Though Pitch's argument-from-experience works well with the herb doctor, allowing him to growl down spongy hypotheses with hard, cold facts, his deep-hid humanity betrays him to the man with the brass plate, and in the end he invests in his dubious wares. But no sooner has the man disappeared than Pitch begins to doubt the wisdom of his action, and when Frank Goodman appears he surlily turns him away, returning once again to his castle of protective misanthropy.

No other character in the story has this pivotal function, suggesting that Pitch is an exceptional example. His position at the center of the narrative, along with his balanced character (at once guarded but warm), indicates that he is the ethical ideal of the book, "good" because vulnerable, "wise" because partly successful in rebuffing the confidence man. In Pitch's closely guarded philanthropy, Melville once again presents the only solution to the threats of a pickpocket world. Only by sewing up his heart in bearskins can a man keep his soul inviolate. Pitch is a malcontent, but he transcends the type, becoming a sort of Kent in coonskins. In his balance, he is to the invalid Titan what Ishmael is to Ahab. It is his defeat which brings the novel to the threshold of tragedy, for when human weakness (the province of satire) results from the faults of a noble heart, when hardness is the armor of a generous soul, then we are in the province of pathos.

When Frank Goodman appears, it is to hold the stage for the remainder of the book, suggesting that he, like Pitch, is an exceptionally important character. Though assuredly a charlatan, he is a knave of finer qualities than those who have preceded him. His friendliness and humble forbearance under insult are more admirable alternatives to the others' obsequious remonstrances, and when he tells Pitch that "this mistaking of your man should teach you how you may mistake all men" (p. 157), the statement, in its very indirectness, contains more truth than the retorts of the early confidence men. Frank Goodman, however much we may doubt his intentions, is an "ambassador from the human race," and to spurn his fraternity is to spurn mankind. Had Melville not prepared for his entrance by the parade of charlatans which preceded him, the reader would have a difficult time understanding what Frank Goodman is all about. *The Confidence-Man,* despite claims to the contrary, is not intended to be read backwards as well as forwards.

Something of Goodman's superior quality is demonstrated by his encounter with Charlie Noble, the unsavory Mississippi "operator" whom he coolly dissects, for Noble is to Goodman what confidence is to charity—a cheap imitation, a parody. By contrast, Mark Winsome, the mystic with the "preternaturally cold, gemmy glance" whom Goodman next encounters, is by far the coolest customer that the confidence man meets. The mystic's appreciation of pure discourse without complications of human indebtedness is perfect proof against the confidence man's appeals to humanity, and he is to be classed, in this regard, with the "bears." But the imperfection of his "system" is revealed when a "crazy beggar, asking alms under the form of peddling a rhapsodical tract, composed by himself, and setting forth his claims to some rhapsodical apostleship" approaches. The cosmopolitan reacts with a charitable gesture and a kind word, while the mystic clinks his ice water indifferently, "more like a cold prism than ever. . . . His whole air said: 'Nothing from me'" (p. 219). Charity for beggars finds no room on the tax form of ethical utility, and Winsome joins Plotinus Plinlimmon in Melville's gallery of heartless idealists. Preferable by far is the invalid Titan's agonized denunciation.

Chief evidence of the heartlessness of Winsome's philosophy is his "disciple," who resembles "one of those wire men from a toy snuffbox," an automaton having "a countenance of that neuter sort, which, in repose, is neither prepossessing nor disagreeable; so that it seemed quite uncertain how he would turn out" (p. 225). The master seems "a kind of cross between a Yankee peddler and a Tartar priest," but the disciple, with "his sharp nose and shaved chin," is pure Yankee, or perhaps something carved by one, and "the last person in the world that one would take for the disciple of any transcendental philosophy." A product of Yankee ingenuity, Egbert has a simple solution to the problem of worldly inconsistency—a consistent expediency.

Perhaps the great irony of this complexly ironic book is that Frank Goodman's facetious cheer is sufficient to betray the hollowness of Egbert's philosophy, summed up in the belief that "the enmity lies couched in the friendship, just as the ruin in the relief" (p. 228). To Frank's hypothetical plea for "Help!" the hypothetical "Charlie" returns a chillingly expedient life preserver, a cypher-shaped "How foolish a cry, when to implore help, is itself the proof of undesert of it" (p. 232). As the first Charlie —whose exploded chicanery resulted in a "Go to the devil, sir!"—denounced jolly Frank, now it is Frank's turn to dismiss the second "Charlie": "What your illustrious magian has taught you, any poor, old, broken-down, heart-shrunken dandy might have lisped. Pray, leave me, and take with you the last dregs of your inhuman philosophy" (p. 253). Proteus seems caught at last, trapped within the "mutability of humanity," and yet the trap, in encompassing man's multifariousness, strangles his essential humanity.

The contrast between the philosophies of Mark Winsome and Frank Goodman, like the encounter between Goodman and Pitch, contains the central paradox of the book. In Winsome we have the calculating coldness necessary for protection against the confidence game, and in Goodman we have the genial warmth by which the game is perpetrated. We admire Winsome's Yankee shrewdness but detest his heartlessness; we cannot deny the importance of benevolence, and yet shudder at the uses to which the confidence man seems to be putting it. By means of these counterpointed alternatives, Melville constructs a static arrangement of antitheses, a ring from which there would seem to be no escape. If "something further may follow of this Masquerade," it can only serve to widen the ring, not break it.

Chapter Nine

The Endurance of Form:
Melville's Poetry

If Melville's poetry, as one critic has observed, is chiefly distinguished by its "differences," it nonetheless shares with his
prose a common basis of form. In *Clarel,* for example, Melville
returned to the cyclical voyage, structuring a wandering symposium, a multipurposed quest which ends, like *Mardi,* with the
death of the protagonist's love and the extinguishing of his faith.
Battle-Pieces presents a more difficult problem of alignment with
Melville's diagram because of its apparent randomness, but the
author seems to have regarded it as an organic "round," which,
by its very miscellany, approaches the summary unity of his various symposia. And in the long poem, "A Scout Toward Aldie,"
he returned once again to the linear quest.

Melville's introductory note to *Battle-Pieces* emphasizes the
organic principle by which the poems are grouped, the writing of
them having "originated in an impulse," their composition having
occurred "without reference to collective arrangement," and the
grouping having assumed a natural order. The title suggests a
gallery of pictures organized loosely about a theme, and Melville
explicitly compares himself to a wind harp, a familiar analogy for
the organicist imagination. The collection represents "the aspects
which the strife as a memory assumes," a collective recollection "as
manifold as are the moods of involuntary mediation—moods

variable, and at times widely at variance." Like "The Encantadas," the poems are unified by the narrating intelligence and provide a spectrum of complementary and antithetical attitudes.

The majority of the poems are short pieces, each dominated by one easily defined attitude, such as the celebration of heroism ("Lyon"), expressions of mourning ("On the Slain at Chickamauga"), or wry observations on the conduct of the war and its effects upon the participants ("A Utilitarian View of the Monitor's Fight," "The College Colonel"). But Melville's poems, like his sketches, are seldom one-dimensional. However brief, they are animated by a controlling contrast or correspondence which allows an ironic or parabolic interpretation. We see young men marching off to death, modern warfare repressing the heroic principle, the celebrated victor as a once disgraced leader. In a few of the longer poems, paradox broadens into noncommitment, a balanced, dramatic view of the conflict, as in "Donelson," a tour de force of objective montage. By means of versified news bulletins, headlines, dramatic dialogue, and impassive description of the changing mood of the crowd that gathers daily to read the war news, Melville frames the puzzling tensions of wartime, the "mysteries dumbly sealed." And in his prose "Supplement," the author recommends a similarly balanced course of reconstruction, a moderate program enhanced by a cautious style: "In times like the present, one who desires to be impartially just in the expression of his views, moves as among sword-points presented on every side" (BP, p. 202).

Ironic balance terminating in noncommitment, in silence, is the chief characteristic of this collection, established in the preludelike "Portent," which heads it. Though Melville wrote the poem in retrospect, he holds himself back from the sermonic advantages of hindsight, and, instead of preaching on the hanged John Brown (his "old foible"), he invests the pendulumlike body with a weight of cryptic prophesy. The corpse hangs from the "beam," suggesting the scales of justice ("such the law"), and like the veiled future of Shenandoah, the "anguish" of Brown's face is concealed. Through hints of diction and imagery Melville suggests the meaning of the hanged man: the skeletal "gaunt shadow on [the] green," the "cut . . . on the crown," the unhealed wounds. These images of death, justice, revenge, and suffering apply both to John Brown and to the veiled future of which he is a portent.

Though Melville often devotes entire poems to the celebration of individual victories and acts of heroism, a number of the *Battle-Pieces* express misgivings about the war. Thus "The Conflict of Convictions" (a title suggesting the author's own "conflict") expresses his fear that the war will destroy "the world's fairest hope" in destroying "man's foulest crime," that democracy will end with slavery, giving way to the "weedy grass" of mobocracy. Yet the poem ends in balance, created by "Heaven's ominous silence over all." The wisdom of cycles tells us that "Age after age shall be/As age after age has been." God, the supreme ironist, takes no side in the struggle, but keeps "the middle way."

In the poems, as in Melville's prose, God's neutrality has its equivalent in the ambivalence of nature. Thus "Donelson" ends, like *Moby-Dick*, with the use of water imagery to suggest the combined themes of eradication and resolution. The gentle but persistent forces of nature reestablish themselves after (and over) the scenes of war, covering the former battleground. Still another aspect of nature dominates "A Requiem for Soldiers Lost in Ocean Transports," in which the surface of the ocean resembles the coming of springtime, while beneath the waves of the "delightsome sea," drowned men are carried "down the pale stream . . . to the reef of bones." In "Malvern Hill," Melville juxtaposes the travail and agony of men and the silent witness of nature by means of rhetorical questions and answers addressed to the elms of the hill. The trees, nature's spokesmen, remember everything but celebrate no one thing. Over "Shiloh" fly swallows, indifferent to the recent struggle of men. In "The Stone Fleet," nature is neutral, "nobody's ally," a power of silence and solitude, an after-quiet of perfect passiveness which provides no answers. As in "The Armies of the Wilderness," the battle remains "A riddle of death of which the slain / Sole solvers are." In *Moby-Dick*, also, death answers all inquiries, but the attitude towards death has changed significantly, from Ishmael's appreciation of Solomon's wisdom to the poet's assumption of it. Like "The Wilderness," Melville remains silent. "Obscure as the wood, the entangled rhyme / But hints at the maze of war—."

Because it follows the quest pattern, the longish "Scout Toward Aldie" is perhaps the best guide to Melville's changing attitude, his increasing disengagement from absolutes. The quest here is a search-and-destroy expedition by a scouting party into the Virginia countryside. The object of the foray is the almost legendary guerrilla fighter, Mosby (coincidentally, "Moby" with an *s*), who lurks in the "green dark" of the forest. Like the Whale, his rumored presence inspires fear and suspicion, and few have seen him "except the maimed ones or the low." Made "every thing" by rumor, Mosby inhabits a paranoiac terrain, enchanted ground, a silent, haunted wood. "A satyr's child," this modern Satyrane dwells in a Spenserian "Eerie Land," where "fire-flies showed with fairy gleam." As in Melville's other enchanted territories, all things are ambiguous, uncertain, illusory.

The scouting party that ventures into this bewitched country is led by a young bridegroom colonel and a battle-weary major, each a variation on Melville's familiar quester types. The colonel is a Pierre-like enthusiast, the major a wise, experienced skeptic. In them "Hope and Experience sage did meet," like sire and son, only with the superior rank given to the son. Both men are brave soldiers, but the major has suffered "through the Seven Days," and has gained the wisdom of pain. Taking solace from his pipe, he remains silent as the young colonel rambles on about "frays in which he meant to beat." As he talks, his companion's eye falls on a gloomy, "moon-tinged" tree, "with crook'd boughs rent or lopped," from which a sinister bit of ropelike bark hangs pendant.

The imagery (and contrast) recalls the terrain in "The Piazza" or the inquisitional furniture in "Benito Cereno," and here, as there, it is designed to qualify the quester's optimism and good cheer. The country through which hope and experience ride is full of similar mementos of death, a wasteland of obscure threat: "drear" and "worn-out fields," "grassed ruins," a decayed chapel pointed to by the plant called "dead-man's hand." Passing from this deathly intervale, they move into "a wood where once tobacco grew / Drowsily in the hazy air," the soporific atmosphere which produces a calm in "all kind things," much as the sight of *Rover* relaxes the kind Amasa Delano: "Such influence . . . bids disarm."

Impervious to the landscape, the colonel "seeks peril" and gets a wry response from the major, who grotesquely writhes his neck to show a buckshot scar—"Kind Mosby's Christmas gift." Scars, for Melville, are invariably the token of bitter experience, and the major, like maimed Ahab, has been bitten by life. But he is no insane, pipe-abjuring monomaniac. He retains the wisdom of the wounded but keeps from madness. Scarred, but sticking to his pipe, he maintains his sanity amid a universe of threat, his attitude a species of protective irony—like Ishmael's, a token of spiritual and intellectual balance. Optimism, enthusiasm, and absolutism are expressed by the colonel, whose faith is as shiny (and untried) as his sword. While questioning a heavily-veiled rebel lady whom his scouts have taken into custody, he insists on playing gallant host and dismisses any possibility of deception on the part of her "Negro" servant with a Delano-like, "Pooh! pooh! his simple heart I see— / A faithful servant."

But the "lady" has a Duessa-like

> glance of mingled foul and fair;
> Sad patience in a proud disdain,
> And more than quietude.

Her "black" coachman is also suspect, for the narrator never calls him a Negro, only "the hump-back," and his deformed body and "yellowish wool like tow" (the absence of punctuation produces further ambiguity—his wool is like tow, or his tow is like wool) recalls the masquerading Black Guinea. The "wool" turns up soon after the lady and her servant are set free, for following an ambush by Mosby's men that kills the colonel, the major finds a wig dropped by a "humped" attacker that turns his thoughts back to the lady and her "black" driver. He never solves the puzzle ("Women (like Mosby) mystify"), but the intimation seems clear.

As in "Benito Cereno," the meaning of the poem is expressed through contrast and paradox, as well as by an atmosphere of threat, betrayal, and latent violence that is resolved by a sudden, brief encounter. The hopeful ride out, watched by cripples in a hospital tent, and the dreary return provide the terms of ironic, diagrammatic balance. Though the colonel is heedless even in death ("Careless of Mosby he lay—in a charm!"), the scouting party is greatly affected by their experience. Returning with their dead and wounded, they bear the "stamp of Mosby," the mark of encounter. Symbolic of the change is the hospital steward. Having ridden out sitting lightly on his mount, secure in the knowledge that his caduceus badge protected him from Mosby, he returns with a "hearse-black" beard and a "heavy heart": "His grape was now a raisin dry: / 'Tis Mosby's homily—*Man must die.*"

II

Battle-Pieces resembles "The Encantadas" in being a static round, while "A Scout Toward Aldie"—taken alone—is like "Benito Cereno" in its domination by a linear element, the futile quest. In *Clarel*, Melville's novel-length narrative poem, both dimensions of the ironic diagram are found. There is once again a voyage out which becomes a full circle ending in death, and the voyage—a pilgrimage—is qualified by a symposium of philosophical dialogues. The pilgrim-philosophers, though more complexly realized than the colonel or the major, fall into similar categories: optimist and pessimist, believer and doubter, neophyte and veteran. And in both poems, significantly, the action consists in the riding out of a "scouting party" into an enchanted wasteland, an atmosphere compounded of danger and death, and both end on a somber, cheerless note. That the same can be said of *Mardi*, *Moby-Dick*, and "Benito Cereno" suggests the unity of Melville's vision.

Entirely missing here, however, is the heroic emphasis of the earlier works, or any suggestion of first-person participation. As in "A Scout Toward Aldie," Melville chooses an omniscient voice, one which urges and manipulates action but seldom intrudes with a heavily rhetorical reminder of authorship and never openly reveals sympathy with any one of the band of pilgrims. That several of the characters voice Melville's own opinions and doubts seems clear (Rolfe, in particular, appears to be a self-portrait), but the author maintains a constant distance from them all, revealing his attitude towards them through indirect allusion and imagery. By maintaining a pose of aloofness and an atmosphere of mystery, Melville enhances the enigmatic implications of his diagram.

Clarel also shares with "A Scout Toward Aldie" the tetrameter line, but whereas its use in the earlier poem is dictated by the ballad form, its presence in the later seems at first wrongheaded. The example of Chaucer, to say nothing of Spenser (heavily relied upon for imagery by Melville), Milton, Wordsworth, and Tennyson, should have demonstrated the propriety of pentameter for a long, narrative-philosophical poem. That Melville was skilled in its use is demonstrated by "The House-Top" (in *Battle-Pieces*) and his magnificent "Epilogue," perhaps the most frequently quoted excerpt from *Clarel*. But, as some critics have pointed out, the tetrameter line seems particularly suited to *Clarel*, for the warped, uncomfortable syntax and the frequent obscurities dictated by the confining four-stresses fit the mood of the poem, their hobbled pace—like the parenthetical style of *The Confidence-Man* (another frustrated pilgrimage)—acting as a brake on the forward movement of the narrative.

The predominance of tetrameter throughout, moreover, seems implicitly to qualify the easy flow of the final lines, with their affirmative burden, the hope that "Even death may prove unreal at the last, / And stoics be astounded into heaven." Very little that has gone before would seem to warrant such optimism. More suitable to the tone of the poem is Clarel's final despair as he wends his way (in tetrameter) down "dusked Olivet" and "vanishes in the obscurer town," an ending which recalls the conclusion of *The Confidence-Man* or the story of Hunilla. Like the Epilogue to *Moby-Dick*, with its convenient, too pat "resurrection," the emerging "from the last whelming sea" in *Clarel* seems factitious. The pentameters, with their Wordsworthian associations, along with the Longfellow-like "sign o' the cross—*the spirit above the dust!*", seem belied by the increasing somberness of the foregoing tetrameters, burdened by doubt and death. In its previous manifestations, the cross has stood for lifeless religion, and its evocation here as a symbol of hope seems forced, if sincere. Still, like Ishmael at the sperm tubs, the pose is nonetheless meaningful for being half-fraudulent. We may perhaps discount the cross, but we cannot dismiss Melville's evocation of "the crocus budding through the snow" and the "swimmer rising from the deep," symbols of affirmation which have their counterparts throughout his works.

If the ending of *Clarel* recalls *Moby-Dick*, so does the beginning. In both stories a young quester has a series of encounters that qualify his projected pilgrimage. Clarel puts up at an inn kept by a black Jew who has returned to Jerusalem to die, next meets Celio, a hunchback Roman who has lost his faith and is also soon to die, and is befriended by Nehemiah, whose senile, dreamy piety is symbolic of dying Christianity. Ishmael's ill-fated "marriage" to Queequeg is paralleled by Clarel's engagement to Ruth, the daughter of the Yankee apostate, Nathan, whose death necessitates Ruth's seclusion and determines Clarel to set out on his pilgrimage. This deathly overture also incorporates the Armenian funeral which Clarel passes as he leaves the city—a sight that is to be recalled several times during the journey, and always in association with thoughts of Ruth, who is also to be the bride of "that Blue-Beard, Cruel Death" (Part I, canto xliii, line 23). Clarel's

pilgrimage ends at her grave, his faith interred with her body. The
death of Celio, the unbeliever, is the first in a series that ends with
the death of Clarel's faith. Commencing at Christ's tomb and
ending at the grave of Ruth, Clarel's pilgrimage is a closed circle
of negation along whose periphery lie the graves of Nathan,
Nehemiah, and Mortmain.

A counterpart to this theme is the mood of alienation, of separation and estrangement. The dead Armenian girl, Ruth, and even
her mother, Agar (Jewish, though American-born), feel homesick
for their native lands. They, Clarel, and the other pilgrims are
strangers in a strange land, having left "home and each familiar
way." They are strangers to each other also, and no two of the
pilgrims are able to reach lasting agreement or accord, their
estrangement epitomized by Clarel's failure to hold "true com-
munion" with the pilgrim to which he is at first attracted, the
mysterious, handsome Vine.

These themes of death and alienation have atmospheric and
imagistic counterparts: the three words "dust," "stone," and "death"
appear frequently during the open cantos, and the landscape
through which the pilgrims ride is a deathly, dusty, and stony
desert. The travelers twice cross Kedron ("importing anguish
hard on death"), and their conversations return persistently
to the death of religions, customs, and past hopes. The first leg of
their voyage terminates at the Dead Sea, in which the faithful,
simple Nehemiah drowns, and towards the end of the return
journey, after a final "night ride," the pilgrims approach the valley
of Hinnom,

> Oppressive, roofed with awful skies
> Whose stars like silver nail-heads gleam
> Which stud some lid over lifeless eyes,

an image presaging the deathly climax to come. As the pilgrims
stand on the banks of the Dead Sea, the water is tinted by a
rainbow, which the priest, Derwent, compares to "The rose upon
the coffin," a symbol of hope, but the cynical scientist, Margoth,

points out that the sea contains the remains of Sodom, punished by a wrathful God. Moreover, the bow soon disappears, leaving a "glazed monotony," causing Clarel to turn for solace to thoughts of Ruth, only to remember the Armenian bier. Significantly, the images of the coffinlike Dead Sea and the tomblike Valley of Death appear at the same place within their respective parts (II and IV, canto xxix, line 151), hinting at the implications of the round. The Dead Sea marks the point of pivot and return, and the valley is the dreary terminus where Clarel discovers why Ruth's image has so often been coupled in his imagination with "dreams of the bier Armenian."

The nihilistic atmosphere is given occasional relief, as when the pilgrims join in song on the banks of the Jordan, bathed in sudden sunshine. But this brief moment—like the bow over the Dead Sea—is "a transient, an esthetic glow" (II. xxiv. 63) which only serves to enforce the atmosphere of denial. These fleeting moments of relief are climaxed by a night of drinking and song spent within the fortresslike monastery, Mar Saba, a scene of apparent "revelry and boon companionship," but which (like the bachelor's dinner) is framed by an atmosphere of denial and death which comes to an end when it is interrupted by a wailing prayer to Christ for mercy, a sound which arrests the five revelers, freezing them like the "problematic shapes" engraved on Greek sarcophagi (III. xiv. 139-43). This image, taking its meaning from the presence of drink and song within a monastery (Greek, like the sarcophagi), opposes the transient joys of life with the permanent fact of death: "Man must die."

The contrast of life and death, hope and despair, becomes a conflict in the opposition of Derwent and Mortmain, antithetical characters whose antagonism recalls the confidence man and his malcontent adversaries. Like the confidence man, Derwent is an advocate of easy benevolence, continually (according to Mortmain) "trying to cheerfulize Christ's moan" (III. vi. 143). He has the confidence man's love of friendship and wine, his liberal views, and his evasion of gloomy thoughts—put off with protesting "Oh, oh's" or a rapid change of subject. He is given to "private and confidential" glances at Clarel, and his private interview with his clerical counterpart, the young theological student, is entitled "In Confidence."

There are not, however, any satanic or serpentine associations in the portrait of the equivocal priest, nor is he given an opportunity to display a Falsgrave-like nonbenevolence. His cheer, though shallow optimism, is harmless enough. And, as if to even the balance, the "sterling" Rolfe early declares that he "likes" the bubbly priest (II. xxxii. 99), a friendly regard which seems to remain consistent until the end (IV. xi. 32). No character, how-ever, may be accepted as representing an absolute value. Though foolish and empty, Derwent is kind, and Rolfe, though wise, has his blind spots. When Mortmain first denounces the priest, Rolfe chides him as "too earnest" (II. iii. 185), yet earnestness is Rolfe's own worst fault, and, during the revels in Mar Saba, the percep-tive Vine notices that Rolfe and Mortmain have matching profiles, "though one looked like a statue dead" (III. xi. 229). Rolfe is to Mortmain what Ishmael is to Ahab, or what Pitch is to the bearded, invalid Titan, or a skeptic to an outright cynic. He can "look a smile" in the face of absolute blackness, "likes" cheery optimism, and often, in his earnestness, makes mistaken judgments.

Though the narrator refrains from solving the puzzle of Mort-main's antipathy towards Derwent, Melville hints at the solution through diction and imagery. The priest is depicted as riding with "light rein slackly drawn," his glance "skimming" over everything, "chirruping" and "patting" his horse, his pleasantness

> Suffused . . . with a prosperous look,
> That bordered vanity, but took
> Fair color as from ruddy heart.
>
> (II. i. 17–28)

The key phrase here, as so often in Melville's (and Spenser's) satiric portraits, is "*as* from," which is not the same as "from." His "fair color" is reflected in the pages of a book he carries, a book of rosy tints and views which suggest the color through which he views all things. Like Falsgrave, Derwent evinces "youth in years mature," riding light as "effervescent foam," and dressed in a light cloth cape and "An easy set of cleric coat." His suit is an emblem of "that facile wit, / Which suits the age—a happy fit."

The deeper implication of this imagery emerges as the narrative progresses, for Derwent's continual shying away from any mention of death ("that ill word / Whose first is D and last is H"), his persistent placing of roses on coffins, his stated love of life and worship of rainbows, is nothing more than an evasion, a refusal to come to terms with the only verifiable truth of existence, "Mosby's homily." On the tower of Mar Saba with Clarel, Derwent gives intimate expression to his shallow latitudinarianism: "Be not extreme. Midway is best" (III. xxi. 283). The balance of Derwent's philosophy is the antithesis of Rolfe's, for it is not a skeptical acceptance of all things but an equivocal recommendation of those things which do not cause discomfort—an avoidance of extremes. Like the confidence man, and for much the same reasons,

> Derwent bred distrust
> Heavier than came from Mortmain's thrust
> Into the cloud—profounder far
> Than Achor's glen with ominous scar.
>
> (III. xxi. 69–72)

Mortmain's "thrust into the cloud" is the counterpart to Ahab's thrust through the mask. He dwells on things below the surface, down in "the slime / Of nature's rudiments and lime" (II. xxxvi. 97–98), commanding the water-colorist Derwent to "Leave thy carmine" colors (III. vi. 140). Whereas Derwent is figured in terms of light and froth, Mortmain is compared to the complex "penetralia" of "Piranezi's rarer prints." Like them, he contains "interiors measurelessly strange" (II. xxxv. 1–2). Where Derwent is described in terms of reflecting surfaces, Mortmain has a "heart, with labyrinths replete," whose "freaks of intimation" reveal Paul's "mystery of iniquity." His character, like that mystery, is "Obscured . . . with prudential haze" and is all the greater for being thus sublime (II. xxxv. 25–30). Idealist turned cynic—maimed by life—he nonetheless retains his desire to believe: a soarer as well as a diver, he gains the "topmost crag" near Mar Saba, so high that an eagle steals his cap, an incident which echoes Ahab's prophetic loss. Like Ahab also, Mortmain is a living skeleton who sleeps "coiled in plight" (III. xv. 17) and seems one of the damned. Yet he is judged innocent by two spirits who hover over him on the shores of the Dead Sea (II. xxxvi. 118–30). When he dies, he is found with his eyes fixed on the symbolic palm above Mar Saba, an eagle's feather on his lips (III. xxxii).

The contrast between Derwent and Mortmain is the most significant of many such antitheses, each contributing to the planetary arrangement of characters and opinions. Divided among themselves, their discussions often break down into arguments, a division which also dominates the imagery associated with the pilgrims and the dreary landscape across which they are riding. The desert is "Direful yet holy—blest though banned" (II. xi. 94), the battlefield of an

> Armageddon,
> Betwixt the good and ill . . .
> But ending in a battle drawn,
> Victory undetermined.
>
> (III. i. 42–45)

In the "many-sided" Rolfe, Clarel sees the "brain and heart's impulsive counter-change" (II. xxi. 137), and he discovers to his dismay that Vine's cool reserve is combined with a "nameless look" of inner weakness (III. vii. 17). In the expedient Derwent, according to Rolfe, "Things all diverse . . . would unite: / His idol's an hermaphrodite" (III. xvi. 176–77). Ultimately, ironically, though each of the pilgrims contains a marriage of contrasts, they are unable to comprehend the vision of a Syrian monk whom they encounter, who reconciles antitheses with a

simple acquiescence: "Thought's extremes agree," no more than
they can penetrate Djalea's monolithic "No God there is but God"
(II. xviii. 142; III. xv. 117). Their individual failures to comprehend the wholeness of life are tokened by the futility of their
quest: that the pilgrimage is a type of voyage is indicated by the
sea imagery which dominates the metaphors throughout. But there
is no final goal, no destination: the voyage out is a complete circle,
a static configuration, and the surviving travelers return
unchanged.

Each of the pilgrims is part of the whole, a representative means
of maintaining (or losing) a perilous outpost of sanity in a self-
contradictory world. Each makes his appeal, mute or open, to
Clarel, but in the end he finds himself with fewer answers than
when he began his journey. The most admirable pilgrim seems to
be the "sterling" Rolfe, who counsels frankness sweetened with
indulgence, fraternity, and tolerance (III. xvi. 217–18)—advice
which resembles Ishmael's generous humanity—and it is to Rolfe,
finally, that Clarel finds himself drawn. But at the end of the
journey, Rolfe disappears with the others, leaving Clarel alone in
his grief of loss. "Keep thy heart," he is told, but we have no sign
that Clarel has even come close to "the issues there." Perhaps,
Melville seems to be implying, he has—like Taji—just begun his
quest, for the numbing loss of faith and Ruth is the sort of burden
which Melville's truth-seekers bear. Perhaps something of Mortmain's mystery is revealed by the story of Clarel's tragedy.

Though the voyage is one of loss, not gain, the sum of oppositions produces a certain wholeness. The contraries that no one of
the pilgrims is able to reconcile are, by their presence in *Clarel*,
fitted "like tenon into mortice," producing a puzzlelike totality, the
"firstling" joined to the "finality" in a diagram of "thought's
extremes" (II. xviii. 139–45), an equivalent of the seamless
totality described in Melville's short poem "Greek Masonry."
Rounded by death and centered by mystery, imbued with an
atmosphere of denial and frustration, *Clarel* is at once a totality
and a cipher, a restatement of Melville's suspicion that "our souls

are like those orphans whose unwedded mothers die in bearing them: the secret of our paternity lies in their grave, and we must there to learn it" (*MD*, p. 487).

III

Further evidence of the endurance of form in Melville's late work is found in the two poems "At the Hostelry" and "Naples in the Time of Bomba," both of which belong to the collection of "Burgundy Club" Sketches that Melville left unfinished at his death. For the poems are late examples of the diptych form: joined at a common base by a concern with Garibaldi and the unification of Italy, they branch out in opposing if not antithetical directions, the one depicting the joys of drink and good conversation, the other confronting, though indirectly, the threat of the "Red Flag" of revolution. Characteristically, "At the Hostelry" is a round, a symposium, which takes its form from dialogues about a common subject, while "Naples in the Time of Bomba" is a linear quest, organized about the wanderings of an American tourist through an Italian city ruled by the tyrant Bomba.

Style in the "Burgundy Club" Sketches is a blend of techniques. The prose pieces, narrated by an anonymous member of the "club," are garrulous and warmhearted in tone, reminiscent of "I and My Chimney," while the poems are dramatic monologues narrated by the Marquis de Grandvin and Major Jack Gentian, two of the club's members. In "At the Hostelry," the monologue is a minor element, for the poem consists largely of dialogues between the various artists gathered around a table. Point of view in the prose portraits is typical of Melville's late work, for the narrator states his intention to remain "where I belong, that is to say in the background." And in the dramatic monologues, this withdrawal is even more marked, although the Marquis, Jack, and a number of the artists voice Melville's favorite themes. The effect, nonetheless, is of complete objectivity, and it is only by means of imagery and allusion that the author suggests with whom his sympathies lie. Like the "author" of *The Confidence-Man* and *Clarel,* the narrator professes to let his characters "talk, sing, and speak as in his own proper person," keeping himself out of the conversations entirely and obtruding only through self-conscious headnotes, somewhat reminiscent of the chapter titles in *The Confidence-Man.*

The Marquis de Grandvin, as his name suggests, is a Haw-thornesque personification of wine. As early as *Mardi,* Melville used the joys of wine as a token of evanescent happiness, and, though the Marquis is praised for his "spontaneous emanations," for inspiring "gentle charities, brave conceptions, heroic virtues," there is something reminiscent of the confidence man about him: "How transitory these prodigal improvident ones can prove!—and once gone, how soon all but good as forgotten!" Though "the talismanic something in the sort of nature here indicated can operate upon another nature though of a temper not favourably disposed to receive its benign influence," once the "talisman" is removed, the beneficent effect disappears also.

Since it is the marquis' genial influence which presides at the table in "At the Hostelry," events there are dominated by a point of view which maintains Derwent's philosophy that "In best of worlds if all's not bright, / Allow, the shadow's chased by light." But as with the genial lawyer in "Bartleby," the marquis is a complex amalgam. Despite his pervasive benignity, he early ex-presses fears that the democratization and modernization of Italy, while having undeniable benefits, will perhaps destroy the beauty which Bomba, through neglect, allows to remain. These senti-ments are distinctly Melville's own, late equivalents of his fear of the "Iron Hand" in the *Battle-Pieces* and the "Red Flag" in *Clarel.* But the marquis' answer to such problems is to take refuge in wine and good company, a refuge which, like the "Bachelor's" haven, is illusory.

If point of view in "At the Hostelry" takes an ironic cast from the marquis' divided attitude, the structure is similarly para-doxical, made up of opposed viewpoints expressed by the artists as to the true meaning of "the Picturesque." The participants are Browning-like historical personae ("Frater Lippi," "Jan Steen," "Spagnoletto," "Swanevelt," etc.). It is soon apparent that a choice of the proper subject matter of art reveals an attitude toward life, and each of the banqueters becomes a spokesman for a familiar Melvillean position. As in *The Confidence-Man* and *Clarel*, representative men are brought into direct confrontation, here while seated around a table—forming a literal round. On the one side, there are those of the party of serenity, earthly joy, and universal benignity, such as Swanevelt, Brouwer, and Fra Lippi. Opposing them are the "silent" ones, Rembrandt, Leonardo, and Durer, as well as the splenetic, misanthropic Spagnoletto, another of Melville's bearish malcontents: "a man of brawn / Tho' stumpt in stature."

Mellow balance is suggested by the genial skepticism of Jan Steen, "Jan o' the Inn," who "dashes with fun art's canvas of truth." Jan's attitude is close to the median that Melville recommended through (and in) Ishmael and Rolfe. Though he keeps a tavern, under his vineyard there is a cave, the tavern-cavern rhyme suggesting the breadth of his philosophy, the coupleted "wine and brine" of earthly existence. For him, *all* subjects are "picturesque." His sentiments draw a well-bred glance of surprise from Veronese, "To mark a prodigal so profound," controlled astonishment which recalls Vine's supercilious attitude towards the earnest Rolfe. Jan's good-natured wisdom opposes the Mortmain-like bitterness of Spagnoletto, but like Rolfe and Mortmain they are closer to each other (and the truth) than the condescending Veronese realizes.

But even the "superb gentleman from Verona" has something of value to offer, and his facetious opinion that the Grand Canal will be drained to serve "This cabbage *Utility*," serves to draw from the company a ring of typical attitudes:

> Pleased Brouwer gave a porpoise-snort,
> A trunk-nose Triton trumping glee.
> Claude was but moved to smile in thought;

> The while Velasques, seldom free,
> Kept council with himself sedate,
> Isled in his ruffed Castilian state,
> Viewing as from aloft the mien
> Of Hals hilarious, Lippi, Steen,
> In chorus frolicking back the mirth
> Of Brouwer, careless child of earth;
> Salvator Rosa posing nigh
> With sombre-proud satiric eye.

From the table of attitudes one may be chosen, but the poem, as it stands, is a static configuration of antitheses, a carefully arranged diagram. Each reader, like Melville, may have his favorites among the artists, but to make such a choice is to deny the apparent relativity of the whole, the perfect democracy of form. And yet circles are as illusory as lines. The marquis may have temporarily escaped his earlier fears through wine and conversation, but he must eventually return to them. And Melville makes his preferences known through tone (overstatement regarding the "splenetic" Spagnoletto, understatement regarding the gentlemanly Veronese) and imagery. As the company reacts to the remark of Veronese, Leonardo is "lost in dream," studying the pink refraction of light through a glass of wine ("The subtle brain, convolved in snare, / Inferring and over-refining there"), while Michael Angelo sits withdrawn and is compared by the mocking Brouwer to the Sphinx, unmoved "by rays of sunny wine." Both artists, the one by his mute study of the pink glow "on the polished table bright," and the other by his preference for water, bread, and the "pale lymph of fame," suggest the evanescence of the joys of life, the illusoriness of the bond of fellowship, the uselessness of chatter to the purposes of true art.

Counterpart to the broken circle is the baffled line, and the progress of Jack Gentian through Naples is qualified by the usual planetary system of counterpointed episodes and characters. Characteristically, the poem opens with a thematic episode, a prelude which dictates the pattern of action to follow. Jack rides through a crowd which has gathered to watch a harlequin tumbler, a mountebank who makes way for him with a bow. Gentleman Jack returns the salutation, causing "a spontaneous demonstration more to be prized by an appreciative recipient than the freedom of the city of New Jerusalem." The initial parting of the crowd is repeated two more times, and each incident is compared, explicitly or implicitly, to the happy occasion inspired by Jack's democratic graciousness. The oppressive march of Bomba's troops causes a sullen drawing back, a contrast to the "spontaneous demonstration" around Jack's carriage, and the passage of a priest and four boys on their way to a deathbed inspires "consent of strange accord." Though the people "part, and in expectation stand," it is not "as men who mirth await." Laughing for Jack, sullen before the troops, the crowd strikes a neutral attitude as the priest goes by, a numbness of superstition without faith.

The dividing crowds are balanced by gathering crowds, at the center of which is always some entertainer—harlequin, juggler, or street singer—whose merriment inadequately conceals the angry mutterings of discontent, suggesting to Jack that even the "ragamuffs cutting pranks" are not "mirth's true elation," but a "patched despair, / Bravery in tatters debonair." The idea of strained merriment, like the theme of dividing and gathering crowds, is contained in the first episode also, for the clowning of the harlequin suggests a martyrdom to joy:

> Reversed in stature, legs aloft,
> And hobbling jigs on hands for heels—
> Gazed up with blood-shot brow that told
> The tension of that nimble play—
> Gazed up as martyred Peter might.

In a way crippled by his contortions, the harlequin resembles St. Peter, who was crucified upside down: mirth in Naples is achieved only through great agony of effort.

The counterpart to the continual harlequinade is the endless religious "holiday" provided by Roman Catholicism, where "feast follows festa thro' the year," a mirthless show tokened by the reaction of the crowd to the priest on his way to a deathbed. The themes of false gaiety, threat, latent violence, and ever-present death are brought together by Jack's reflections on the side of Pausilippo, the "seat for pleasurists" which lies between Bomba's fort and Vesuvius, "two threatening bombardiers." Where one represents temporal tyranny, the other is a token of ever-present death, bringing to mind "funeral urns of time antique / Inwrought with flowers in gala play." The urns are associated by Jack with Naples, both old and new:

> Yes, round these curved volcanic shores,
> Vined urn of ashes, bed on bed,
> Abandonment as thoughtless pours
> As when the revelling pagan led.

The major's tour of Naples is an initiation, marked by his gradual awakening from the belief that "True freedom is to be care-free! / And care-free seem the people here." The symbol of his dying illusion is a rosebud presented to him by "a flying Peri" early in the afternoon. The rose is a token of euphoria, like wine: "Flushed with the rose's reflex bloom, / I dwelt no more on things amiss." Each time Jack gives his mind to "thoughts less cheerful then archaic, he is checked by a sportive sally from the Rose." Whenever he ponders a "discouraging fact," he is "twitted by the festive Mentor." His visit to Pausilippo brings this opposition to a head, for when his reflections on mortality cause his brow to droop, the glory of "the red red ruddy and royal Rose" expands into full bloom to chide his melancholy.

Momentarily a token of joy, an expression of *carpe diem*, the rose soon joins the vined urn as a *memento mori*. When the cry of a girl selling "blood-oranges" inspires prophetic visions of "incensed Revolt" and "Pandemonium's red parade," the rose—now in dusty full bloom—is unable to respond, and as the afternoon passes it begins to lose its petals. The first falls when the arrival of Bomba's troops puts an end to the satiric ballad of a street singer, and the last when the deathbed priest comes by, his presence bringing all things to a silent halt, the crowd frozen like

> . . . Pompeiian masquers caught
> With fluttering garb in act of flight,
> For ages glued in deadly drift.

Keyed by these images of death, the close of the poem is a "catafalque," a "ringing down the curtain on the Rose." As in "The Piazza," "when the curtain falls, truth comes in with darkness." There are few sermons, but Jack Gentian gradually becomes aware of what is happening in Naples. And yet, like Naples, he is trapped between extremes—he can draw no conclusions, only a curtain:

> Let bide; nor all the piece esteem
> A medley mad of each extreme;
> Since, in those days, gyved Naples, stung
> By tickling tantalising pain,
> Like tried St. Anthony giddy hung
> Betwixt the tittering hussies twain.

Despite the demurrer, the poem is indeed a "medley of each extreme," a composition of antitheses whose terms, in their very contrariety, put forth a puzzling consistency.

Chapter Ten

Final Balance:
The Prose Fragments and *Billy Budd*

In his last poems, Melville continued to be concerned with the themes and images of his earlier work, particularly *Moby-Dick*. Thus "The Berg," with its passive, inscrutable monster of ice, recalls the blank whiteness of the Whale, while the image of the "slumbering kraken" in "The Aeolian Harp"—actually a drifting hulk—looks back to the horrible squid of Chapter 59. The fate-dogged "Admiral of the White" in "The Haglets" resembles Ahab in finding death in victory, his fate a compound of themes suggesting hope and doom, life and death. "The Enthusiast" demonstrates that Melville was still capable of championing Quixotes, and "The Enviable Isles" suggests the pastoral vision that dominates Ishmael's consciousness. The lighter side of Melville's vacillating vision is represented by "Herba Santa"—tribute to the blessed relief of tobacco—and its companion piece, "Magian Wine." And, in the stoical "Pebbles," Melville once again demonstrates the all in all of nature, at once a destroyer and a healer, a "dragon" and a "dove."

As various as the *Battle-Pieces*, *John Marr and Other Sailors* and *Timoleon* reflect the mind of a man who could neither believe nor disbelieve. Much like Melville's Civil War poems, many of the individual pieces are invested with ironic contrast, an ever-present sense of paradox: unrequited love, victory ending in death, unrecognized worth, the treachery of appearances. And yet these last works differ somewhat in tone from the earlier, for the subject matter seems invested with a detectable mood of acquiescence if not acceptance. If the themes seem borrowed from *Moby-Dick*, the tone is traceable to certain of the prose sketches of the 1850's. Like "The Encantadas," "The Piazza," or "I and My Chimney," they lack the anger, the smothered rage, of his heroic romances and seem to take their mood from Ishmael's occasional fits of stoicism. And in the "flower" poems of his last years, Melville seems especially to have surrendered to a stoic faith in nature, abandoning despair for a calmer mood. There, the vernal impulse of life seems to compensate for the ultimate void which it screens. Candide-like, Melville appears to have ended his own quest with a willingness to tend his garden.

Thus, "The Rose Farmer," a dramatic monologue spoken by an old man who has inherited a rose farm, who has "come to his roses late," would seem to be an autobiographical statement, a key to the implication of the other flower pieces. But, as the use of a rose in "Naples in the Time of Bomba" suggests, that flower carries a temporal incense, the odor of mortality, and there are certain hints even in the rosiest of his last poems that Melville may have regarded warm hues still as a trick of light, that his roses were not without their thorns. Such, at least, is the implication of a prose fragment written at about the same time as his flower pieces, whose very title, "Under the Rose," hints at the hushed revelations of a confessional.

The dominant symbol of this sketch is an amber bowl used by a Persian Azem, to hold roses of many colors, which fall in such a way as to conceal "certain *relievos*" carved into the amber. The chief of these carvings "under the roses" is "a round device of sculpture . . . showing the figure of an angel with a spade under arm like a gardener, and bearing roses in a pot; and a like angel-figure, clad like a cellarer, and with a wine-jar on his shoulder; and these two angels, side by side, pacing toward a meagre wight, very doleful and Job-like, squatted hard by a sepulchre, as meditating thereon; and all done very lively in small." The meaning of this "round device" is suggested by the amber in which it is carved, which contains the tiny corpses of insects, each in its "dainty little skeleton chamber." Lurking beneath the roses like the Dead Sea beneath the reflections of a rainbow, or the "millions of strange, cankerous worms" concealed in the "starry bloom" by the piazza, the dead insects are a persistent reminder of mortality.

Like the doubloon in *Moby-Dick*, this round device contains a static balance of attitudes: the Job-like meditator on death; the gardener bearing roses, suggesting both hope and mortality; and the cellarer, bearing the wine of escape and forgetfulness. As the three peaks on the doubloon are joined by a common base of darkness, so the figures are carved into the catacomb of amber, and both angels bear a significant token of death, a spade and an urn. Here, as in "A Scout toward Aldie" and *Clarel,* the uninscribed motto seems to be *"Man must die!"*

Notably, the devices on Ahab's doubloon are emblematic of attitudes towards life—ethical and ontological—whereas the relievo suggests attitudes towards death. Though in all of Melville's important works death is regarded as the final answer to the question of life, as the coefficient of whiteness and silence, the answer is often forgotten in the tremendous kineticism of the quest, the forward rush of Melville's seekers. In the *Battle-Pieces,* however, we can see the emphasis changing, for it is difficult to think on war without dwelling on death, and in *Clarel* the hero's slow, painful search is weighed down with the evidence of mortality. In these later works, also, the linear element—the register of vitalism —virtually disappears, and the dominant configuration becomes a closed circle of opposed contraries. As in "A Scout toward Aldie" and *Clarel,* the line of the quest becomes a circle, corroborating Ishmael's view, not Ahab's. And in the end the circle remains unbroken, there being no romantic Tajis to break through it into an infinity of speculation.

Like the doubloon, the "round *relievo"* is studied by several persons, and each regards it differently. The rich Azem who owns the vase accepts its message stoically; a poet is inspired to write a cryptic song, opposing "Death's open secret" with a Montaigne-like, "Well, we are"; a visiting ambassador to whom the vase is shown becomes "sadly distraught"; and his servant, the narrator of the poem, reacts with pleasure to what he takes to be the "profane capering" of the mountebank poet. In his last work, similarly, Melville provides opportunity for a range of choices, for though the dominant theme is death, the rose light at times becomes so intense that it resembles a nimbus. Yet there is sure to be a grave-sitter for every rose farmer and winebibber, and the golden amber of style is often found to be full of deathly images.

II

Death for Melville's romantic heroes is a final act of self-assertion. Their isolation self-willed, Taji, Ahab, and Pierre are alone, yet hardly lonely. But commencing with "Bartleby," Melville began to associate death with abandonment, with enforced isolation and estrangement. *Israel Potter,* in so many ways the antithesis of Melville's romances, emphasizes the victim-hero's unwilling alien-ation, his final loneliness and death, and it is this novel, perhaps more than the other writings of Melville's "middle" period, which looks forward to the work of his last years. Not only does it share with "Daniel Orme," "John Marr," and "Rip Van Winkle's Lilac" themes of old age and isolation, but certain passages presage the style of these last sketches as well. This is particularly true of the opening chapter, where the prose is highly rhythmic, taking its movement from a counterpoint of antitheses: the change of seasons, the passage of time, the cycle of birth and death, the solace of memories during present hardship. Such a style differs markedly from the baroque rhetoric of *Moby-Dick* or the neoclas-sic facetiousness of *The Confidence-Man.* The point of view seems detached, yet the mood is infinitely compassionate, like nature herself.

The balanced style of this opening chapter evokes a peace and harmony which is to be lost by Israel forever. In the sketches, however, the style is consistent throughout, its balance promoting a static quality which emphasizes the condition of the central characters—each is in some way imprisoned by conditions, held from participation in life. Like Israel Potter held in by the walls of London, they somewhat resemble the dying King Lear. They are generally depicted as motionless, fixed in posture of meditation or deliberation, like the Job figure in the relievo. Only in "Rip's Lilac" is there any physical motion, but here it is a bewildered return which is anything but a quest, like Israel's last visit to his birthplace, an unwilling discovery that his home has disappeared. Like the "burnt-out" Ahab before his last hunt, or "alien Israel" in London, these isolatos are soothed by "tender but quenchless memories," whose persistence suggests (and is compared to) the ever-returning greenness of nature.

An exception is the Donjalolo-like Rammon, a youth engaged in an intellectual search for truth. But such a search is inevitably carried out in isolation, and Melville points out that "isolation is the mother of illusion," the lesson of those solipsists, Ahab and Pierre. Rammon is imprisoned within his self, like all of Melville's earlier questers after the absolute. Because of his bookish quest, he contains a shadow of Captain Vere and links the earlier quester-captain to the late. Like Vere (and Ahab), he is important as a demonstration of the relation of man to the wholeness presented to his perceptions by nature. And it is perhaps significant that "Rammon" is an unfinished fragment, that Melville's finished work of this period is more concerned with the presentation of mysteries than with the frustration of those who try to solve them.

Thus, Daniel Orme is virtually mystery itself. Like the mysterious Mortmain, he is one of Melville's "bears," a lineal descendant of Nord and the ancient mastman in *White-Jacket*. Gloomy, silent, and secretive, like Ahab he is compared to a hibernating grizzly, sucking his own paws for solace, "his coat the worse for wear, grim in his last den awaiting the last hour." At sea, he shuns his fellow sailors, spending his days below decks sleeping between cannon, and when he retires to the land he keeps "a quiet, leonine droop about the angles of his mouth, that said—*hands off.*" Unlike John Marr, a sailor landlocked among strangers on the prairie, Daniel Orme is a willing pariah, presumably driven to solitary ways by the pangs of past misfortune or guilt.

Like Mortmain, Orme represents the "mystery of iniquity." He comes from "no imaginable sphere," like a meteor (or Bartleby), and though all men have their say about him, no one knows who he is or what he has been. The style of the sketch is correspondingly allusive and obscure. In the opening paragraphs, instead of talking directly about Orme, the narrator alludes to "a character," "a sailor," only gradually introducing "the old man-of-war's man," ambivalence which prepares for the sly, elliptical passages to follow: "Whatever his disposition may originally have been, never, in his latter cruises at least, had he been specially noted for his sociability." Like Daniel Orme himself, such a style is largely made up of blanks: conjectures, qualifications, parentheses.

Some clue to Orme's past is provided by his talismanic tattoo, "a crucifix in indigo and vermilion" worn "on the side of the heart," a cross marred by "a whitish scar long and thin, such as might ensue from the slash of a cutlass imperfectly parried or dodged." In contrast to the cross borne by Israel Potter, which is formed entirely of battle scars and is a token of his maiming encounter with the world, Daniel's cross is broken by a scar, suggesting some assault on his faith imperfectly "parried." But the narrator refuses himself omniscience, retreating behind conjecture: "Even admitting that there was something dark that he chose to keep to himself, what then? Such reticence may sometimes be more for the sake of others than one's self."

Like his tattoo, Orme's death is emblematic. On shipboard, Daniel found a hermitage between cannon, and his deathbed ashore is "an obsolete battery of rusty guns." He is found leaning against the cannon, "his legs stretched out before him; his clay pipe broken in twain; the vacant bowl and no spillings from it attesting that the pipe had been smoked out to the last of its contents. He faced the outlet to the ocean. The eyes were open, still containing in death the vital glance fixed on the hazy waters and the dim-seen sails coming and going or at anchor nearer by." The posture recalls Mortmain's death stare at the palm, and Orme's death on Easter Day hints at some vague religious significance as well. In the poem "Pebbles," the "inhuman Sea" is praised as a universal balm, "Distilled in wholesome dew named rosemarine." "Orm"—the philosopher, not the sailor—is mentioned in this poem, connecting it with the sketch and warranting the narrator's guess that "he fell asleep recalling through the haze of memory many a far-off scene of the wide world's beauty, dreamily suggested by the hazy waters lying before him" that he died in peace, not pain.

Rosemarine is another name for "rosemary," a token of "remembrance" and of "healing presence." When Orme is buried, it is in "a lonely plot overgrown with wild eglantine," a flower (sweetbriar) emblematic of "poetry" and of "wounding to heal," almost exact synonyms for "remembrance" and "healing presence." Like the sea-washed pebbles, Orme seems to have been cured (smoothed) by that which wounded him, to have accepted the dragon and the dove, the eternal collision of sea and land. He is found on the beach, not (like Agatha) because he is to become a victim of grinding forces, but because (like Hunilla) he has been polished by them. He has learned the lesson of the shore: "The Seas have inspired it, and Truth— / Truth, varying from sameness never."

But this positive note is qualified, like Melville's other affirmative statements, by a series of questions: "What had been his last thoughts? If aught of reality lurked in the rumors concerning him, had remorse, had penitence any place in those thoughts? Or was there just nothing of either?" The old sailor, like the druids with whom he is associated, is a mystery unto the end, his talisman the broken cross and pipe and the wild eglantine on his grave. Was he "just nothing"? His mystery remains unexplained at the last, his final "peace" only one of many conjectures.

As in "Daniel Orme," the structure and style of "Rip's Lilac" are dictated by theme, here not the blank mystery of isolation and the slyness of inkept secrets, but the mysterious round of nature's rhythms. The focus is not on the central character, Rip, but on the processes which he and the lilac represent. Whereas the development in "Daniel Orme" is simple, limited merely to his mysterious story, "Rip's Lilac" has several narrative lines, or movements, each in some way involving the natural processes of growth and decay. A harmonious prelude to this pattern is the lengthy dedication to the "happy Shade" of Washington Irving, described as "reclining . . . under the golden maples," an image suggesting autumnal ease, but referring specifically to Irving's grave. "Happy Shade" evokes the shadow cast by a living tree as well as a benign spirit, and, like other "mellowing Immortals," Irving lives on through his works, "sharing fame's Indian Summer." In the sketch which follows, this theme of life-after-death dominates a complex pattern, in which life springs from death, beauty from disorder, recognition from amazement, a metaphorical enjambment recalling Melville's review of Hawthorne's *Mosses*.

The first movement of the sketch begins with Rip's "resurrection," in which the dazed and bewildered old man returns home from his long sleep on the mountain to find a giant lilac growing by his doorstep, where once a willow grew. Like the palm in *Clarel*, the lilac testifies to the processes of rejuvenation, a vegetable equivalent of Rip's awakening. The history of the decaying house near which it grows provides the second movement of the story and is also identified closely with Rip, a token of his disorderly past life, "in a condition rather slatternly as to externals." The "slatternly" house and happy-go-lucky Rip were the cause of early antagonism between him and his bride, who, hating old age as much as disorder, wanted to get rid of the ancient willow by the doorstep. Like the domineering wife in "I and My Chimney," she is on the side of newness and progress. Despite her persistent complaints, the uncompleted ("arrested") house and the weeping willow remain as they were, harmonious counterparts of natural disorder, decay, and death.

The third movement commences with a description of the willow's death. Toppling from old age and becoming in time a gravelike mound "with wild violets springing from it here and there," the willow is succeeded by the lilac, and, as the lilac grows, the house decays, its decline harmonizing with the blooming promise of the lilac, providing a picturesque sight which a young artist chooses as a subject for a painting. The fourth movement of the story is a dialogue between the painter and a "gaunt, hatchet-faced, stony-eyed" Calvinist, who wants the artist to paint " 'something respectable, or, better, something godly; paint our new tabernacle—there is it,' pointing right ahead to a rectangular edifice stark on a bare hillside, with an aspiring wooden steeple." The crude linearism of the building and its finger-pointing advocate are a contrast to the "leisurely decay" of Rip's cottage, with its lovely "gay screen" of lilac. The hatchet-faced man attacks the lilac for being "half-rotten" (as Rip's wife earlier attacked the willow), but it is he who reminds the artist of death on a pale horse, while his gleaming white church reminds him of a "cadaver." Natural disorder, which is the cyclical harmony of decay bringing forth life, is preferable to mankind's artificial "order," his mechanistic, "rectangular" (linear) drive towards newness and precision.

The final movement of the sketch, in preparation for the initial stanzas of verse to follow, returns to Rip, "in his picturesque resurrection bewildered and at a stand [like the lilac] before his own door, even as erewhile we left him." The round suggested by this return to Rip takes its shape from the cycle of nature, containing repeated images of arrested growth, old age, death, decay, rebirth—all warranted by the original legend of Rip Van Winkle. Nature here is neither the blank apathy of the prairie which surrounds John Marr nor the dragon dove of the ocean. It is the "redeeming attractiveness" of the Catskills, an affirmative harmony of death-into-life. The "useless" lilac, planted by the "useless" Rip, becomes an object of veneration and pilgrimage: "See, where man finds in man no use, / Boon Nature finds one—Heaven be blest!"

"Inhuman Nature" has become "Boon Nature," but the succession is not absolute, unless we are to assume that Melville gained a final optimism in the last few years of his life. Rather, "Pebbles" and "Rip's Lilac" may be taken as descriptions of aspects of nature, rather than developing stages of Melville's attitude towards nature. In both, as in "Daniel Orme," nature puts forth a type of solace, relative to place and circumstances. Moreover, by reading "Rip's Lilac" backwards, as it were, a darker implication can be made to appear. It is, after all, out of the mold of a dead tree that the lilac grows, and the "gay screen" over the "tenantless ruin" of the house is like the roses which hide the catacomb bowl. If nature provides solace, it is in the consolation found in Melville's lovely poem, "Pontoosuce," where the song of "waning and waxing" ends on the refrain "All dies!"—the motto of Mosby and *Clarel*. Nature's kiss smells of the grave, and her presence contains the "warmth and chill of wedded life and death." Death may promote life, but the lilac is not the willow, and Rip's resurrection is not eternal. Even the letters of his name (*R.I.P.*) contain a hint of the final peace which will soon claim him, the same rest enjoyed by the Happy Shade of his creator, the silent place in which all secrets are kept.

III

Billy Budd is generic to Melville's other late works, the poems and fragments discussed above. Like Rip's lilac it springs out of them, quite literally, for the mysterious old Dansker was salvaged from the portrait of Daniel Orme, and it is he, the story intimates, who alone understands Claggart's behavior towards the inoffensive "Baby" Budd. The flower poems are also evoked, for Billy's name contains the budding lily of purity, and the concern of "Rip's Lilac" with man's insistence on imposing squares on nature's heedless round is the major theme of the story, here transposed into martial versus natural law. And like so much of Melville's last work, the narrative is slow-paced, ponderous, the fable weighed down with conjecture, hypothesis, qualification. Its ending, with the double deaths of Billy and his judge, Captain Vere, is still another affirmation of Mosby's motto.

Yet in some ways *Billy Budd* seems different from much of the later work, less "mysterious," even didactic. Though more complex because it is longer, its issues seem somewhat simplified, and, though the opposition of Christly Billy and Satanic Claggart is surely diagrammatic, it appears almost melodramatic in its reduction of values. Only Captain Vere seems to give the story complexity, his deliberations acting like a balance wheel in a watch, preventing a rapid, obvious resolution of the action. Without Vere, it might be said, the story would only be concerned with the mystery of Evil. With him, it becomes involved as well with the mystery of Good. It is Vere's decision, and the debatable rationale for it, which introduces the complexity of intimation, the ambiguity which is typical of Melville's planetary structures.

Still, considering Melville's earlier concern—particularly in *Clarel*—with diagrammatic characters as well as structures, it may be a mistake to consider Vere the only complex creation in the narrative. The possibility of additional complexity may be derived from a comparison of *Billy Budd* and "Bartleby," for Captain Vere resembles the lawyer of that story. Confronted by the purity of innocence and the purity of malevolence, Vere ignores absolute considerations for relative ones, while yet appealing to absolute (though temporal) order. Like the lawyer, he plays a sorrowing Pilate, in whom is found a matching of both head and heart, rational action and human sympathies. Like the lawyer, the captain owes his allegiance to the temporal world, while Billy—like the scrivener—seems to have descended from other realms.

Yet Billy shares little with Bartleby save an alliterative "B." Where one is pallid and drawn, the other is rosy and tanned; where one is wasted and reclusive, the other is full-bodied and gregarious. Bartleby seems the personification of Death, Billy like

Life itself, the vital urge incarnate. It is his very attractiveness which has drawn so many readers to the story, as the "Handsome Sailor" himself captivates so many of his companions. But "handsome is as handsome does," and Billy is a more ambiguous creation than his appearance suggests. There is in the portrait a lower layer, like the subpigmentation in Leonardo's paintings, a certain whiteness under the rose-glow of health. Something about him, for instance, recalls the Marquis de Grandvin, that "golden wine . . . in a golden chalice." Like the marquis, he possesses qualities of "the unvitiated Adam," a great "physical beauty" coupled with "moral charm." Like him also, he has a "talismanic something," a nature which "can operate upon another nature though of a temper not favourably disposed to receive its benign influence." It is this aspect of Billy, resembling as it does the transitory effects of wine, which hints at his fragile hold on life, his resemblance to the flower his name connotes.

To understand this is in some way to understand Claggart's mysterious hatred of the beautiful Billy. Like Jackson's hatred of Redburn, it is comparable to Satan's envy of Adam and Eve, the spite of the damned towards the innocent. Redburn claims that Jackson envies his youth and good looks, but fatuous ass that he is, he grasps only the obvious. "If askance [Claggart] eyed the good looks, cheery health, and frank enjoyment of young life in Billy Budd, it was because these went along with a nature that, as Claggart magnetically felt, had in its simplicity never willed malice or experienced the reactionary bite of that serpent" (p. 78). Despite his apparent inhumanity, Claggart is more intensely mortal than his genial adversary.

During the trial, Vere dismisses Claggart's malice as a "mystery of iniquity," an apparent rationalization for the sake of expediency, but the narrator also uses this phrase in connection with the master-at-arms (p. 76). The phrase recalls Mortmain, in *Clarel*, linking Claggart even more firmly to Melville's "admirable" haters, and ultimately to Ahab: "Toward the accomplishment of an aim which in wantonness of atrocity would seem to partake of the insane, he will direct a cool judgment sagacious and sound. These men are madmen, and of the most dangerous sort, for their lunacy is not continuous, but occasional, evoked by some special object" (p. 76). Claggart's regard for Billy is like Ahab's hatred for the Whale, or like the antipathy of Mortmain towards the rosy Derwent; it is like Spagnoletto's hostility towards Fra Lippo Lippi, or the fury of the one-legged misanthrope towards the bland peddler of confidence. It is "an antipathy spontaneous and profound such as is evoked in certain exceptional mortals by the mere aspect of some other mortal, however harmless he may be, . . . called forth by this very harmlessness itself" (p. 74). This is the scorn of darkness for the silly illusions of daylight, "cynic disdain, disdain of innocence—to be nothing more than innocent!" (p. 78). Though a figure of "elemental evil . . . like the scorpion for which the Creator alone is responsible," Claggart's poison is the stinging serum of truth. In *Clarel*, the gentle victim of life, Agath, shrinks away with a cry of fright from a "crabbed scorpion," an "unblest, small, evil thing," which Rolfe calls a "small epitome of devil."

> "Wert thou an ox couldst thou thus sway?
> No, disproportionate is evil
> In influence. *Evil* do I say?
> But speak not evil of the evil:
> Evil and good they braided play
> Into one cord."
>
> (IV. iv. 24–29)

A human scorpion, Claggart yearns to sting Billy with an awareness of the essential malignity of earthly life, and though his method is evil, his intentions are not entirely so.

For Billy Budd is a representative of the serenity that was, for Melville as for Swift, the "felicity of being well deceived"; like Captain Delano he is a natural innocent, a noddy whose primitive composition makes him incapable of detecting deceit. He trusts all men, accepts appearances for what they seem, and is even foolish enough to think that he can become friends with the man who hates him most. This quality of perfect innocence inspires "grim internal merriment" in the old Dansker, whose "eccentric un-sentimental old sapience, primitive in its kind" as Billy's inno-cence, "saw or thought it saw something which in contrast to the warship's environment looked oddly incongruous in the Handsome Sailor" (p. 70). The Dansker, like Claggart, is of the party of darkness. Where the master-at-arms is a stalking cat, the Dansker is an owl, and both see things that even Captain Vere is blind to. The warship world is the world-warship, a mechanism whose imperfection is compensated by a delicate system of balances—like the lawyer's office in "Bartleby"—and in which there is no place for perfect innocence. Billy is not of this world and does not stay long in it. A heavenly Christ, he does not have a sufficient weight of earth. His antithesis, Claggart, is entirely of clay, while Captain Vere—the man in the middle—contains a balance of parts. It is he who is the mortal Christ, who takes upon himself the responsi-bility for his fellow men.

Again, however, Melville's diagram is a system of qualifications: as Billy's unearthliness is qualified by his mortal stammer, so Captain Vere's sense of justness is too much reliant upon the convenience of (linear) forms. And if Claggart's dark vision in some way redeems him, the redemption takes place deep in the shadow of the rose. With Billy at one extreme and Claggart at the other, the three characters seem to present a gauge of mortality, ranging from absolute good to absolute evil, but the values repre-sented by each undergo subtle shifts as the action progresses. As in *Pierre*, the parts revolve in a synchronized movement, so that when absolute good becomes relative evil it is confronting relative good. Lacking the linear thrust of the quester, *Billy Budd* is a "round," containing a microcosmic inclusiveness and governed by a movement in which places are exchanged like "the laughing couples down a country dance." With Melville's other rounds, it results in a cipher, a "mystery of iniquity" in which Billy is the victim, Claggart the instrument, and Captain Vere—with all his Roman love of the general good—the expedient perpetrator.

Despite the formal implications of ironic balance, it would be a mistake to assume that Melville attained a "final peace" in his last novel. Although the massive materials and movements of *Moby-Dick* are missing, the constant exchange of values suggests a corresponding restlessness. The diagrammatic complexity of characterization and the parenthetical, conjectural style, with its studied distaste for open declarations, are a subtle counterpart to the great counterthrusts of characters and styles in *Moby-Dick*. And in both books the implications of form are similar, for the drastic reduction of the linear element has not altered the meaning of the dominant, all-encompassing circle. Withdrawing behind dramatic opposition and discursive indirection, Melville purposely allows the narrative "to vindicate, as it may, its own credibility" (p. 77). But the method of *Moby-Dick* is similar, despite differences of style, and as early as *White-Jacket*, Melville allowed "Truth to vindicate itself." If Melville abandoned the heroic pose as quixotic, he never seems to have had much faith in it. He has moved his encounter from the operatic backdrop of a whale hunt to the subdued murmur of a courtroom, but his characters are as afloat as ever, drifting in a sea of conjectures.

IV

Though not a quester, in the sense that he *knows* what he is after, Captain Vere resembles Captain Ahab in being an advocate of the linear view. As Ahab puts his faith in charts, so Vere believes that "With mankind . . . forms, measured forms, are everything; and that is the import couched in the story of Orpheus with his lyre spellbinding the wild denizens of the wood" (p. 128). Ahab overlooks the element of chance, and Vere, in considering the effect of forms on mankind, neglects to remember that the "wild denizens" tore Orpheus apart in a frenzy. Captain Vere's forms are political, "applied to the disruption of forms going on across the

Channel and the consequences thereof," and his reliance upon them reflects the same fears of revolution that appear in Melville's work as early as *Mardi*. Though political forms are ultimately illusory, in that they bely the eternal flux of life, they are the only bulwark civilized man has against the chaos that is the opposite extreme. The danger is that form will become formalism—a strict advocacy of "right"—and will attempt to halt the natural, pendulumlike movement by which nature manifests its own balance, to impose a dead balance contrary to that cyclical sway. It is Captain Vere's misfortune that he is called upon by his "time and fate" to effect just such a balance. His execution of Billy, though perfectly just, is perfectly unnatural.

This seems to be the implication of the stateroom in which the trial takes place, a compartment which resembles the lawyer's office in "Bartleby," divided as it is into opposing portholes with a skylight overhead, and at the far end opposed staterooms containing the imprisoned Billy and dead Claggart. The cabin itself is described as "a goodly oblong of length coinciding with the ship's beam" (p. 105), and the word "beam," along with the perfect balance of the arrangements within, suggests the scales of justice. Billy is on one end of the "beam," Claggart on the other. The mechanism is given further complexity by the placing of the court, for Captain Vere, though "sinking his rank" in order to appear as a witness, nonetheless maintains his privileged position on the "weather side" of the "beam," which elevates him above the members of the court, who are seated on the lee side. On the literal level, Vere's position indicates his superior rank, but on the metaphorical level, it signifies the "light" weight of his minority opinion. The balance is decidedly against him, a balance represented both by the opinions of the court—who "naturally" side with Billy—and the pitch of the ship as it contends (like Vere) with natural forces.

Something further of this intimation is hinted by Vere's act of pacing, "in the returning ascent to windward climbing the slant deck in the ship's lee roll, without knowing it symbolizing thus in

his action a mind resolute to surmount difficulties even if against
primitive instincts strong as the wind and the sea" (p. 109). In
walking up the rising deck, Vere's action is symbolic of his attempt to impose balance on the pivoting heave of nature's rhythm,
and by returning to windward each time against the lee roll he is
walking up the steepest incline possible—bucking both wind and
tide. Like Ahab, he is imposing his will on nature, and he will
suffer Ahab's fate.

We are never told in which of the opposing staterooms Billy
and Claggart are placed. Their opposition is important only in
regard to the matter confronting Vere and his court: "In the light
of that martial code whereby it was formally to be judged, innocence and guilt personified in Claggart and Budd in effect
changed places" (p. 103). Vere is neither for nor against Billy; he
is for the dead balance of martial order, the preservation of forms
against the threat of flux. Like his fellow members of the court,
who wish to free Billy because of his essential innocence, Vere
feels the "full force of . . . Nature," but his allegiance is not to
nature, it is to the king—to temporal law. Vere defines his position
as "unnatural," in opposition to the instinctive feelings which
would in a natural situation have acquitted Billy. Billy is "naturally" good as Claggart is "naturally" evil, but Vere stresses the
irrelevance of natural ethics: "Budd's intent or non-intent is
nothing to the purpose. . . . War looks but to the frontage, the
appearance" (p. 112).

Billy, too, has depended on appearances, and his faith in them
eventually leads to his death. Though war "looks but to the
frontage," it becomes the final reality of Billy's situation, as he lies
in chains "between . . . two guns, as nipped in the vice of fate."
The guns are black, a "funereal hue" which contrasts with Billy's
white clothing, compared to "a patch of discolored snow in early
April lingering at some upland cave's black mouth" (pp. 118–19).
The sullied snow is at once an image of Billy's mortality and his
natural purity, a token of the unadulterated primitiveness which
has been somewhat tarnished by "virgin experience of the dia-

bolical incarnate and effective in some men." Like Adam, Billy is doomed by his encounter with the knowledge of evil, and his rosy flesh is evaporating like the snow to which he is compared: "The skeleton in the cheekbone at the point of its angle was just beginning delicately to be defined under the warm-tinted skin" (p. 119).

In contrast to Billy's fragile, natural beauty is the massiveness of the machinery around him, illuminated by the "dirty yellow light" of oil supplied by those who gain profit from "the harvest of death." The "flickering splashes" of artificial light "pollute the pale moonshine all but ineffectually struggling in obstructed flecks through the open ports from which the tampioned cannon protrude" (p. 119), much like the grass that struggles for a hold in the pavement of Bartleby's prison. Above decks, the moon (regulator of "time and tides") is bright and full, its light silvering everything "not blotted by the clear-cut shadows horizontally thrown of fixtures and moving men" (p. 116). Here, as below, man and his objects are linear and fixed, "polluting" and "blotting" the pure light of nature. Even the sailors for whom Billy is to become a sort of Christ govern themselves by "strict adherence to usage," part of the mechanism upon which he is crucified. In their simple way they are given to "forms" as much as their captain.

The third emblematic juxtaposition of law and nature, of fixed forms and fluid rhythm, occurs during Billy's execution: singing his final benediction, the "Handsome Sailor" rises birdlike into the air, his departure timed to coincide with the arrival of the ship at "an even keel," his death a witness of Vere's maintenance of dead balance. "In the pinioned figure arrived at the yard-end, to the wonder of all no motion was apparent, none save that created by the slow roll of the hull in moderate weather, so majestic in a great ship ponderously cannoned" (p. 124). But Billy does not "die." We are never told specifically that he is a man being hung—he "ascends"—and we are not told that he is dead. Indeed, he is still in motion, like a pendulum swinging in time to the roll of the ponderous warship, its "majesty" caught in the pulsating rhythm of nature. The moment of dead balance has been only a moment, and the rhythm continues its rise and fall. The victim is not Billy Budd—it is Captain Vere. When he is blessed by Billy he becomes "rigid as a musket," paralyzed by the "shock" of innocent irony. All his motions are those of a man who has been hung, while Billy, birdlike, ascends.

The reaction of the crew to Billy's death, at first a dumb silence, then "a sound not easily to be verbally rendered," introduces the fourth juxtaposition of law and nature. This sound, the crew's instinctive reaction to the sight they have just witnessed, is the threatening release of emotions which is a sign of man's primitiveness, and it is compared to the "sloping advance through precipitous woods" of "the freshet-wave of a torrent suddenly swelled by pouring showers in tropical mountains." The narrator ironically passes off the "muffled murmur" as "inarticulate," and therefore "dubious in significance further than it seemed to indicate some capricious revulsion of thought or feeling such as mobs ashore are liable to, in the present instance possibly implying a sullen revocation on the men's part of their involuntary echoing of Billy's benediction."

But the narrator's demurrer is weakened by Melville's customary qualifications, the "possibly" and "seemed," and the facetious context of "inarticulate," "sullen," and "capricious." The murmur is sympathetic, like the feelings of the court a natural response, and it is countered by the strategically timed piping of the new watch. Unlikely music, the "silver whistles of the boatswain and his mates" have the Orphic effect of piercing "that ominous low sound [and] dissipating it." The irony is that the music is scarcely the soothing strain that one associates with Orpheus. It is harsh, discordant, "unnatural"—like the system it enforces.

A second and more ominous murmur attends Billy's burial, when the sailors are aroused by the circling of sea birds over the burial spot. But this superstitious reaction (keyed by nature) is not tolerated and is quelled by the drum beat to quarters, "which familiar sound happening at least twice every day, had upon the present occasion a signal peremptoriness in it. True martial discipline long continued superinduces in average man a sort of impulse whose operation at the official word of command much resembles in its promptitude the effect of an instinct" (p. 127). The response, again, is achieved by "music"—forms—but the "instincts" so affected are not natural. They are "a sort of" impulse which "much resembles" instinct but which has been "superinduced"—imposed on man's natural independence.

The consequences and the tenuous sway of such an imposition is suggested by the background of mutiny and revolution against which the narrative is enacted. Vere, the fool of forms, is eventually killed by a bullet fired by a soldier of the French Republic "from a porthole of the enemy's main cabin," the windward counterpart of the porthole from which he stared during Billy's trial. Eventually his advocacy of temporal order is belied by the overruling laws of nature, and the captain dies with Billy's name on his lips. But for a time the forces of form win out, and Billy's death is followed by a reestablishment of order and routine, though with a slight variation, as if somewhat out of focus.

> At this unwonted muster at quarters, all proceeded as at the regular hour. The band on the quarter-deck played a sacred air, after which the chaplain went through the customary morning service. That done, the drum beat the retreat; and toned by music and religious rites subserving the discipline and purposes of war, the men in their wonted orderly manner dispersed to the places allotted them when not at the guns.
>
> And now it was full day. The fleece of low-hanging vapor had vanished, licked up by the sun that late had so glorified it. And the circumambient air in the clearness of its serenity was like smooth white marble in the polished block not yet removed from the marble-dealer's yard.
>
> (p. 128)

These two paragraphs are like a seal upon the ambiguity of the story, for above the formal, ordered activities of man, nature maintains its own order, the cyclical progress of the sun. Rising, the sun disperses the rosy clouds that gave Billy's ascent a seemingly mystical importance, as death has dissipated the rosy healthfulness of the sailor himself. All appearance is a trick of light. A perfect blank remains, "circumambient air" as white and serene as a block of marble hewn from a quarry—an image which contains at once a circle and a square, tokens of nature's round completeness and man's imposition of linear symmetry upon it.

This image, like the unfinished, imperfect narrative which contains it, is a final seal to Melville's many ambiguities. As blank as the Whale, the block of marble is serenely mysterious, latent with or perhaps innocent of particular meaning. Like the new tabernacle in "Rip Van Winkle's Lilac," it is testimony to man's persistence in squaring nature's circle, but the circle cannot be squared, and the block—like all fiction—is artifice, is a lie. Moreover, it is as yet incomplete and awaits the definition of an artist's chisel—some relievo or legend—or perhaps reshaping into an imitation of a natural form. Still, as it stands the marble block most resembles a tombstone, a further hint that only death can provide the symmetry of pure fiction, can solve the final mystery, and it is with the death song of Billy that the story ends, as the chains that bound him to life and law dissolve into the oozy weeds fathoms down.

Index
to Characters and Works